learning to
dance inside

Also by George Fowler

Dance of a Fallen Monk
Feed Your Soul

learning to
dance inside

Getting to the Heart of Meditation

George Fowler

ADDISON-WESLEY PUBLISHING COMPANY

Reading, Massachusetts   Menlo Park, California   New York
Don Mills, Ontario   Harlow, England   Amsterdam
Bonn   Sydney   Singapore   Tokyo   Madrid   San Juan
Paris   Seoul   Milan   Mexico City   Taipei

Library of Congress Cataloging-In-Publication

Fowler, George, 1929-
    Learning to dance inside : getting to the heart of meditation /
    George Fowler.
        p. cm
    ISBN 0-201-41039-7
    1. Meditation. 2. Fowler, George, 1929-   I. Title.
    BL627.F678   1996
    158'.12—dc 20   95-39383
                                                             CIP

Jacket design by Jean Seal
Text design by Merrick Hamilton
Set in 12-point Bembo by Merrick Hamilton

1 2 3 4 5 6 7 8 9-DOH-0099989796
First printing, March 1996

To Lori
with lasting love

———

He who does not dance
does not know what is happening.

———

*From a Gnostic text
uncovered at Nag-Hammadi, Egypt*

CONTENTS

———

ACKNOWLEDGMENTS

———

Through the words of mystics and masters heard over many years, I am aware that I have been provided with what is good about this book. With equal gratitude, I acknowledge my life companion, Lori, and my friends and students who have shared their spiritual energy with me and helped me not underestimate the potential for lighthearted fulfillment that each of us has on this earth.

INTRODUCTION

There are already hundreds of books about meditation, and here comes another. But this one covers the topic in a way different from most.

This book is primarily about the goal of meditation, not about meditation itself. Meditation has value only insofar as it carries us to a contemplative experience. In these pages you will not learn about spiritual techniques, but about achieving freedom from psychological guilt, about finding the dance in your heart, about recognizing your oneness with the universe in a transcendental experience of peace and joy that is traditionally called the contemplative experience, bliss, high consciousness, cosmic consciousness, enlightenment. This book isn't intended to teach you how to meditate as much as it is aimed at helping you find your essential and overwhelming happiness.

Meditation is a way of correcting the fact that human formation customarily teaches our minds to chatter about the world of appearances, but never trains them to give us an adequate grasp of the unseen—and greater—reality in which we live. Meditation is a means of coming to an experience of this greater reality.

The mind would have us believe that what it perceives through the senses is all there is to our universe. Thousands of years of human spiritual experience, however—as well as our own occasional moments of intuition—suggest there is more. Meditation is a way of finding this *more* for ourselves, not by better thinking, but by learning to go beyond the mind and its limitations and to seek a nonconceptual experience of what thought alone has failed to give us.

———

THERE ARE TWO WAYS to go about transcending the mind, that is, to go about meditating. The most commonly taught way is to pursue bodily and mental techniques that slowly quiet the mind so that the experience of what lies beyond its grasp can come forward unhindered and be experienced. According to this method, if the mind concentrates on a mantra, a mandala, or the breath, it will gradually grow quiet and the grand expanse of higher reality will rise to awareness. This way works for many, but it didn't work for me and hasn't for the substantial majority of those whom I've guided over the years in learning to meditate. Some people, myself included, need to have our minds more explicitly involved during the early stages of learning anything new.

I am convinced that a more effective way for most of us to transcend the mind is to beat it at its own game: vigorously involve it at the beginning in gaining spiritual insights and convictions that will, in good time, lure our hearts beyond the limits the mind itself had set for us. When we have sufficiently rethought, expanded, and replaced our mind's presuppositions, our hearts will be moved to look to the transcendent experience that the mind slowly begins to suspect.

This does not mean that the mind will or can ever adequately comprehend or portray Eternal Existence, the Source Being that many call God. But the mind can be filled with new knowledge in place of its assumption that all of reality is visible to it. After its initial shock and complaints, the mind will grow enthusiastic at its new vistas. It is, after all, a part of us; it's on our side. If we have involved it in our enterprise, it will in due time readily fall into silence as it understands that such a course of action (nonaction) is truly to our (and its) benefit. This will be especially noticeable once our heart has begun to dance in response to what the mind has started to parade before it.

———

Meditation is not concentration, nor is contemplation a magnificent montage of beautiful thoughts or new and better convictions. But while contemplation does transcend thinking, it remains an experience that initially and most readily results from more accurate, adequate, and higher insight. A blissful experience of Ultimate Reality will more readily come to us as a result of spiritual insight and broadened understandings than it ever will from the imposition of any degree of bodily and mental discipline we might employ to try to make our customary self grow quiet. *The mind must, indeed, eventually be quieted and transcended*, but this is helped along more surely by replacing the erroneous content about which it is chattering than by making direct efforts to silence or ignore it. You do not get rid of an obsessing thought by concentrating on getting rid of it. You do so by supplanting it with other thoughts.

Nature abhors a vacuum nowhere more than in the human mind. If we try simply to turn the mind off, we have laid an enormous task before ourselves, indeed. Taking the mind along on our journey to bliss is not only easier, but also more often successful. And more quickly so.

———

WHEN WE USE OUR MINDS to rethink our understandings about ourselves, about the cosmos, about God, our new insights lead us beyond mere mental exercise to a growing sense of security, peace, joy. This happy state slowly metamorphoses, without our knowing when or how, into a wordless ecstasy. And this sublime state of ultimate personal fulfillment is alone adequate, in turn, to convince the human race to drop at last its fear-driven competition, its rank greed, its endless squabbling. Only then do the universal compassion required by the Buddha and the no-exceptions love required by Jesus and other spiritual masters become realistically attainable.

1

HOW IT HAPPENED FOR ME

I am a consummate authority on what does *not* work in the practice of meditation. If this book does nothing but help readers avoid the mistaken, starry-eyed practices and false starts that I pursued for many years, I will be satisfied. I intend, though, that it teach its readers to do much more than avoid mistakes.

I became interested in meditation as a senior in high school, but I started meditating consistently and earnestly only the next year when I was an insecure, confused, rowdy—albeit sincere—young submarine sailor in the Philippines. I've told the full story in a previous book, and it's sufficient to say here that by this time in my young life I had ample reason to be frantic in my search for what meditation can supply: reassurance, meaning, security, freedom from psychological guilt. Through conversation with a thoughtful and spiritually inclined fellow submariner and by plunging into spiritual reading, I became firmly and finally convinced that I would find the relief I needed through meditation. Still scared, still deeply confused, I launched into it with a passion even exceeding that with which, until then, I had sought relief in alcohol and other damaging habits.

Five years later, by then a Trappist novice at a monastery high in the mountains of Utah, I was still feverishly trying to meditate, and still largely at sea as to what I was supposed to be doing with five to eight hours a day of Gregorian chant braced by perpetual silence and solitary meditation. During vespers one hot Sunday afternoon in July 1952, my youthful vanity was suddenly and painfully struck by the realization that while I had already been in the monastery for two years, I still wasn't holy. I had given up most of the pleasant things in this world, but had nothing to show for it and was still, I cried out to the universe, not even able to meditate.

How It Happened for Me

Pushed by my own panic, I frantically undertook a reading program to try to remedy the situation and pored through twenty-three books on meditation in the following few weeks. While this reading was driven by a neurotic fear resulting from finding myself to be an inadequate monk, I later came to realize that it did me a lot of good. It helped me understand, early on, that most books about meditation concentrate on techniques of meditating and not on the purpose and goal of meditating. After finishing all of these volumes, I found myself feeling that it would probably be wiser to try to entice the horse into the barn with oats than struggle to get him in with trickery or whips. In other words, might I not move into the contemplative experience of God more surely and more quickly by concentrating on the delightful nature of that longed-for experience than by fixing on the varieties of techniques pushed upon me for getting there?

———

THE PRACTICE OF MEDITATION is not a matter of simply waiting in silence for something wonderful to happen. If for no other reason than to be able to recognize the experience when it does occur, we should deliberately get to work to help it along. *Our chief preoccupation should be not with the way we do it, but with why we do it.*

The conclusion I reached as a result of my smarting vanity and panicked reading was echoed by something I read years later in a book on prayer—the name of which I have long since forgotten—by a British Benedictine abbot, Dom John Chapman: "Pray as you can, not as you can't." I found no small peace as I came to realize that when we set out to meditate, each of us has the task of understanding whatever spiritual principles are involved and of then applying them in our lives *in our own way.* With this clarification of responsibility and freedom, the meditative techniques we use will suit our temperament, our intelligence, our background, and all the other variables of our personal situation.

Most of the authors I read that summer (indeed, as I recall, all of them) were so interested in the *how* of meditation that they didn't spend much time explaining the *what* and *why* of it. With their concentration on techniques, they ended up teaching not much more than bodily discipline and mental prayer (an inner discursiveness as free of distractions as one can make it). My insight gave my efforts to meditate a renewed start, but it would be many more years before I would come to a clear understanding of meditation and of its relationship to contemplation.

I walked away from that summer's compulsive reading experience with the realization that what I wanted was not nonstop encouragement to start meditating—for which I required no urging whatsoever—or a sales pitch for various techniques. What I needed—and didn't find—was a book dedicated to the *understanding* of meditation. I was convinced that if only I could comprehend what was supposed to be going on during meditation, the techniques would take care of themselves.

I was right. This present book is the one I needed and didn't find back then. And this is why I have made specific how-to guidance only a small part of the text and have placed it near its end.

Learning to Dance Inside

———

OUR THOUGHTS AND IMAGINATIONS start out being exactly what Teresa of Avila called them in the sixteenth century, "idiots in our house." Fears, feelings of insecurity, distractions, emotions of a thousand sorts—our inner confusion and inner noise in general—are *not* what we should be concentrating on. My beginner's error and the erroneous guidance of many books on meditation is a preoccupation with trying to control these "idiots." It is far more helpful to *understand* what is amiss in the presuppositions from which they arise. When we have understood that, we are at their root, and they will disappear soon enough by themselves. We will begin to be distracted away from our distractions.

We must *understand* what our options are. We must understand *for ourselves* the nature of the universe and how we fit in. We must come to know clearly what lies beyond the myths and storyforms (the various forms religious stories take) that religions have taught and at which they so often stop. We must bring full awareness to the whole enterprise and to all its underpinnings.

The fallacy of my early attempts at meditation was that I thought of enlightenment as a grand reward to be eventually given to me by a great Heavenly King who generously let me call him Father. I was taught—and was completely confident—that He would reward me if only I could manage to hold my face just right while thinking the prescribed thoughts as I awaited transfer to another world.

That's not at all how the search and finding of ultimate fulfillment, of enlightenment, of contemplation happens.

After seemingly endless trial and error, pretending and hoping, falling and rising again and again, I found I had learned many important things about meditation: guidelines and insights that seminary professors, monastery masters, and countless books failed to teach me. And I have learned many more since.

This present book is about what I learned. It's written so others won't have to take as long to reach their breakthroughs as I did.

2

MEDITATION WORKS

What in the world was Buddha doing sitting day after day in all kinds of weather under that bodhi tree? He obviously wasn't trying to beat Isaac Newton to the punch on the gravity thing, because he was certainly bright enough to know that bodhis don't bear apples.

And what was Jesus doing out there in the desert all night by himself? It was too dark to play solitaire, and if he was just looking for a good place to sleep, there's reason to believe that several of his friends would have taken him in. And there's no evidence whatsoever that he was interested in astronomy.

I could ask what went on in the protracted silent solitudes of any number of the world's spiritual masters and mistresses. (Let's leave it at masters and consider the word to include both men and women.) Why did Zarathustra, for example, stubbornly stay in his tent when the king had a suite done over for him in the palace? What kept Babaji going out there alone in the alternating snow and heat of the Himalayas? And his sister, Mataji—what was a woman doing alone out where tigers wander? And there's Anthony and Muhammad and Ignatius in their respective caves, Teresa of Avila in her bare cell, several Catherines spending all their adult lives happily ensconced behind high walls, and . . . well, *lots* of spiritual giants willingly engaged with solitude everywhere in the world. What really went on in their silences?

Even if we agree with history that all of these spiritual masters were maintaining their silence for specifically religious reasons, it might seem to some readers to be begging the question if I were to suggest that they were busy meditating, or enjoying the fruit of meditation, contemplation. Having lived in silence for seventeen years in a Trappist monastery myself, I know first hand that if anyone remains healthy and perseveres for long periods in silence and solitude, meditation and contemplation are the only adequate explanations.

———

THESE TWO TERMS, meditation and contemplation, need to be clarified now, both because they are core to an understanding of what will be said here and because they are so often misused or erroneously applied interchangeably.

The word *meditate* and its related term *meditation*, as used here, refer to the deliberate practice of the awareness of unperceived, spiritual realities, an awareness that will, if pursued intelligently, lead logically and inevitably to contemplation. As agreed to by the world's spiritual tradition, *meditation is the deliberate practice we undertake in order to come to a contemplative experience of Reality.*

Contemporary use of the words *contemplate* and *contemplation* is more confused still. A person can be said to contemplate a sunset, a fork in the road, next summer's vacation, or exciting new tax strategies. When I was a freshman in high school my father once suggested that I "contemplate" carefully what might result were I to arrive home at 3:00 a.m. yet one more time. As used in this book, contemplation doesn't refer to consideration or reasoning at all. It refers to a state of awareness that is beyond both mental discursiveness and sense perceptions and is composed of what spiritual tradition calls high consciousness, cosmic awareness, enlightenment, and words of similar meaning in many languages. Contemplation must not be thought of as some sort of bizarre state. It is, rather, the sublimely uncomplicated *experience* both of the cosmos and of ourselves in a way that transcends both sense perception and the mind's reasoning. The experience of contemplative bliss is nothing more nor less than the experience of the Oneness of all things, including oneself. As such, the history of the struggle for security, joy, and fulfillment by the human race suggests that when properly understood, contemplation is a human condition matched by no other.

———

WHILE MEDITATION IS THE USUAL WAY to come to the contemplative state, some people can and do come to this high experience without ever having learned to meditate. This should not surprise us. Some people, too, are born musical geniuses and compose symphonies without ever having had to study music. But here's the bad news for any reader who at this point may feel a flicker of hope that he or she can get by without having to make an effort to learn to meditate. Unless you are already an accomplished contemplative, you are one of those who need to learn how to meditate first. If contemplation were destined to come to you without any effort on your part, you'd already have it. You don't really have to use *this* book to study meditation (although this one will go easier on you and will shorten your path), but you do need to learn to meditate somehow. Besides, by the very fact that you picked this book up and didn't walk right by it, you've proved that you're still looking for some degree of fulfillment, and that, therefore, you need to work at learning to meditate.

————

SPIRITUAL MASTERS ARE SIGNIFICANT not only because of the explicit teachings they pass down to us. They're also important because they model for us what it looks like to be a contemplative who is taken up with the grandeur, beauty, and love of that Eternal Being whom many of us call God. Imagine for a moment, if you will, what it must have been like for Jesus out in the desert when he was experiencing the presence and limitless beauty of Eternal Being. Imagine Prince Siddhartha's delight when he finally bestirred himself from under his tree in his new contemplative state of enlightenment and had to announce to his friends that they should henceforth call him Buddha (literally, an awakened one).

This book will help you realize that you are essentially the same as any awakened ones, any enlightened ones. It will help you understand what Jesus meant when he prayed that we might all be, by gaining enlightenment, what he knew himself to be: one with the God he called—and invited us to call—Father. We know that Gautama Buddha achieved enlightenment through meditation: the historical records are explicit about the fact that he attained it while sitting under a tree. Regardless of the contention of traditional Christian theology that Jesus never had to work for his full contemplative realization, many of us believe that he, too, like other Jewish prophets before him, achieved his degree of awareness by the practice of meditation. Exactly as the Buddha did. The important point is that Jesus and all the other spiritual masters did, in fact, realize something that made them supremely happy. They were taken over by a sense of fulfillment, delighted to be here, released from anxiety about the future, and totally free of guilt about the past.

For them, meditation worked singularly well.

3

EXAMPLES OF ITS RESULTS

It's surprising how quickly a little effort to bring the spiritual into one's life can bear fruit. Remarkable fruit. And meditation—spirituality reduced to practice—is the premium way of doing that. In teaching meditation to others, I've many times seen this concrete, practical application of spirituality replace turmoil with peace, change despondency into lightheartedness, put personal pride where there had been only self-rejection, and place a sense of meaning and orientation where before there had been only confusion and self-doubt.

———

FIVE YEARS AGO, a friend of my wife's was told by her psychiatrist that she had to start taking a powerful antidepressant daily if she wanted to get the upper hand on her long-standing personal turmoil. She recounts that after she heard this prescription she went home and sat down with a cup of coffee to review her options. The drug's zombielike side effects didn't appeal to her. As it happened, shortly before receiving this prescription, she had taken a course titled Finding Peace and Joy from a Higher Source. The spiritual guidance she learned in this class seemed the better of her options, and she determined to solve her problems, as she puts it, by meditation, not medication. This approach will not work for everyone because not everyone has this woman's clarity of purpose and strength of resolve. But it certainly did work for her and does for many. If people are foolhardy to dismiss the advice of good physicians—and many are—they are equally foolish to dismiss the option for spiritual healing that is theirs. Each of us is able to engage the power for transformation that is within us, a power we tap through meditation.

This friend has now been meditating for five years. It's evident to all who know her that she has gained control of her life to a remarkable degree.

Typical of many others, she reports that by learning to meditate, she learned how to go within and become aware not only of her Source Being, God, but also of herself. The personal power she came to sense within enabled her to make significant changes without. She started by confronting her husband about his habit of disparaging her: "I know you don't intend to belittle me, but you do, and I'm asking you to go within yourself and ask why you feel the need to speak to me the way you do." Her quiet firmness served as a model for him, and he responded thoughtfully. Their relationship is today dramatically healed. More important still, her attitude toward herself is dramatically healed. Where there had been frantic rush and dabbling in every new kind of therapy and hyped weekend seminar, her present gentle, humor-filled demeanor and active lifestyle speak clearly about her new inner security and her transformation from the psychologically disheveled person she was to the strong and confident person she has become.

———

ANOTHER ACQUAINTANCE who knew only turmoil and self-doubt also undertook a program of daily meditation. After about a year of meditating, she was offered a divisional management position that, her bosses later told her, had already been offered to two men. Both had refused it, saying the division was in such a mess that it could not be salvaged and that its certain failure would look bad on their ré-sumés. They openly chuckled when it was offered to her, but she hesitated only long enough for a quick glance inside herself before saying she'd accept the post. Clean up the mess she did, and she turned her new division completely around in the process. The results were evident to both friends and critics. In eleven months her previously failing division showed its first profit in four years.

What my acquaintance never told anyone but her spiritual guide was where she found both the strength of personal resolve to do what she did and the clarity of purpose with which she did it. She normally began her days at 4:30 a.m. and, with a cup of coffee and a book as her only companions, meditated until 5:30 a.m. (Not many newcomers would be wise to undertake so strong an initial dose.) After a few months of confusion and some floundering, her meditation leveled off and became stable. I especially remember her statement the day she received an award for the success she had made of her division. She smiled as she told me: "How can a person who feels absolutely secure ever really fail in anything?"

———

TIM, WHO DOESN'T MIND if I use his real name, is another example of the power of meditation. He had been deeply dependent on drugs for several years, and had forfeited both his career and family as a result. After turning to meditation and beginning to rebuild his life, he sometimes joked that perhaps now he was as addicted to meditation as he previously had been to drugs. He knew well, however, that what drew him to meditate was the goal of self-respect, the pursuit of a renewed and deepening feeling of security and wholeness. In his early days as a meditator, he often told me that no one knew better than he the dark depths against which any new feeling of happiness could be compared.

He promised himself every day not to forget the Eternal Reality that he had become acquainted with during meditation, and yet the intensity of his work seemed always to cause him to forget it. It's the same for everyone at first, but where Tim was singular was how quickly he came to understand that it doesn't much matter if the realization sensed in meditation is kept in mind or not: the Reality revealed there remains real all the same. "The fact of the Fact is forever a fact" is a mantra even more useful than it tries to be cute. What Tim began experiencing every morning in meditation astonished him, and he realized sooner than most that it would be present with him the rest of the day whether or not his conscious mind remembered it. Virtually every time we got together, he told me that he could hardly believe how beautiful his life had become, a life that less than two years before he had seriously considered ending.

———

HUMANS EVERYWHERE want essentially the same things: happiness, security, a sense of worth and creativity, inner and outer freedom. Even when they decide to go after these goals by meditation, their efforts will be expressed differently in various cultures. Meditation around the world takes a huge number of different forms. But whether in the West or East, within this religious tradition or that—or outside of all religions and merely as a philosophical exercise—meditation of any sort always seeks an identical goal: bliss.

When one embarks upon the practice of meditation, it's helpful to hear about the efforts of others and to have models of how success looks. This "how," however, is not about how others sit or breathe or what they read, but lies in the fact that they take time alone, that they try gently to relax, and that as part of the process they read or otherwise seek to deepen their insights. It means, most of all, that they know they are after an experience, not just a clarified set of beliefs. All who want to meditate must understand that they are each unique and should not simply try to reproduce the meditative methods of others. Be inspired by others' achievements; be cautioned and encouraged by others' modeling, but keep in mind that each of us is functioning with our own specific inheritance of race, culture, formation, and education. We are wise to realize early that the way others meditate and the way they describe how they do it will sometimes be helpful, sometimes counterproductive. It will be an unfortunate detour if we stand more in awe of what others accomplish than of what we ourselves have it in our power to accomplish.

We will be wise, too, to know early that we have as much potential for success at meditation as anyone else in any place or time. If we can't manage that much positive self-assessment, it will be helpful to try to imagine what it would feel like if we could. We do better to start our journey into contemplation using the make-believe of "what would it feel like if" than not to start at all.

—

4

A GLIMPSE OF THE GOAL

When meditation finally worked for me, it wasn't what I'd been taught to expect. The contemplative experience wasn't what the books I'd read on the topic prepared me for, or even what spiritual directors and father masters had promised me in a silence-bound Trappist monastery hidden away in the mountains and dedicated to nothing but the contemplative life.

The difference is this. For years I had been working doggedly at the front door of my spirit, preparing for an eventual, sublime, marriagelike union with an intimate, *but separate,* Divine Being. One day, to my astonishment, I found that the Object of my search had all along been patiently waiting for me, unrecognized, at the center of my house.

The One I had been seeking wasn't a separate Being at all. God not only wasn't somewhere off across the universe, he wasn't even separate here inside of me. God, my Source Being, was present and expressing Itself *as* me.

The One with whom I eventually recognized my oneness, my union, was not the separate God—howsoever loving and attentive—about whom I had been taught since childhood. Instead, and exactly as world mystics and spiritual masters like Plotinus, Meister Eckhart, Paramahansa, Jesus, and the Buddha have been reporting for millennia—something which I and millions like me had obviously not understood—the Supreme Being turned out to be the Eternal Existence present and expressing Itself as my own deepest nature, what some spiritual traditions suggested I call my "Higher Self."

To use a metaphor of Meister Eckhart that cannot be repeated too often, when I was searching for God, I was like a person riding an ox while looking for an ox to ride on.

A Glimpse of the Goal

AS THE CONTEMPLATIVE STATE ADVANCES, it becomes increasingly difficult to explain either the process of how we got where we are or exactly what the experience itself is like. This experience differs so significantly from what the rational mind and human logic expect that neither mind nor its logic can understand or explain it. They have none of their customary points of reference on which to build. Not the least cause of this confusion is the fact that the contemplative experience itself is substantially simpler than that to which our minds are accustomed. It's easier to use metaphors than to try to describe contemplative union with God explicitly. Eventually, however, we do have to try to get beyond metaphors and discover their meanings. If this high state cannot be shared exactly, we must at least tell something about it and about what it feels like.

What is the contemplative state like? It's finding yourself existing, *be*-ing, in a totally different kind of awareness than you've ever known. You have become aware, for the very first time, that you are an eternal "expression" of Existence, or, translating the Latin roots of that word, an "outpressing" of Eternal Existence, of God. When this astonishing realization registers, it becomes at that moment a dance in your spirit, a laughter somewhere inside, a clarity of the mind that is at once the most profound and simplest experience you've ever known, and at the same time the least specific. You feel an overwhelming sense of lightheartedness that sometimes, literally, makes you short of breath.

If what I have just written makes the contemplative state sound unrealistic, then I have expressed myself poorly. Once this state is possessed, it is no more mysterious or strange than meeting an old friend. And it's just as comfortable. It may seem elusive at first, but that's because it's too close for conventional scrutiny. It may make us ill at ease briefly, may even scare us, but that's only because it's unfamiliar.

———

IT'S HELPFUL TO UNDERSTAND from the beginning that there are variables along the route to spiritual breakthrough that should not be given too much attention. How well you can concentrate, for example, is not critical—despite a frequent misconception—or how well you can whip up inner images, or how long you can sit without fidgeting. Visions don't matter; nor do warm feelings, flashing lights, or even, as some report, attending angels. When, in great delight, you are finally aware of the reality of your deepest Being—and of everyone else's—you'll see clearly that all else about your life, by comparison, is incidental.

In the contemplative life and the practice of meditation, beginners will do well not to long for visions, levitations, or any other unusual events that tradition calls extraordinary phenomena. Such happenings are simply not important. If they do occur, the sixteenth-century mystic John Yepes suggests that we move on quickly, for whatever good they were intended to effect was accomplished the moment they happened. Any dalliance over them will be a distraction at least, a service to vanity more probably.

———

LEARNING TO DANCE INSIDE

YOU WILL KNOW that you have arrived in a contemplative experience when one day—effortlessly and usually unexpectedly—you realize that you chop your wood and carry your water (or, replacing those ancient Zen images with ones of the twentieth century, you balance your checkbook and negotiate your commute) exactly as you did before, but now with the joy of knowing that it is the Source Being doing these things *as you*. When it dawns on you that the stars are doing *your* twinkling, you've got the point. When you see it is impossible that you'd ever again take even the subtlest part in bigotry, sexism, or any other illusion of competitive and fear-driven separateness and insecurity, you'll know you have become a meditator and a contemplative.

This is not talk about a passing poetic moment, but about a deep, abiding, and transforming realization, one that is significantly more overwhelming because of being experiential and not just cognitive. When that day comes, you will be astonished at the simplicity of what has happened. You will ask, as everyone with the experience does, how could you have previously viewed something so simple as if it were difficult? You will then realize that if you needed help along the way to find your bliss, it was not so much to learn what to do, but to learn what not to do: not so much where to look, but where to quit looking.

There will be times en route when you will be profoundly absorbed in the spiritual process and will find delight in understanding things more clearly than ever before. Be grateful for these insights, but push on. Don't call them the goal. Call them recollection, insight, progress, consolation, but don't think they constitute contemplative enlightenment. That state is not a thing of the intellect, but of the heart and spirit. It's not an insight, but an experience.

When you feel deep peace, call it peace, not bliss. All meditation is peaceful, but not all peace is the sublime experience of contemplation. Sometimes, after all, our bodies and minds react blissfully over nothing more sublime than a good cheese sandwich, a new twist of logic, or a winning at the racetrack. We must keep our sights elevated, for if we truly want to meditate and to achieve the contemplative experience that is enlightenment, we must be convinced that it is significantly different from any happiness that comes from any kind of fortunate turn of material events.

You are successful at meditating when you *experience* your absolute security and abundance and bliss, and your complete identification with all people and all things. You will then confidently know, without the possibility of a doubt, that the contemplative experience is yours.

In that day your heart will dance, and you will no longer need this book to help you know what to do—or even what not to do.

5

AN OVERVIEW OF THE PROCESS

Meditation is a personal creative experience, not an exercise in conformity. Everyone who meditates successfully will come to the contemplative experience in a way customized to his or her own temperament, personal formation, and store of information and images. It's comforting to know that every individual's experience is just as valid as anybody else's. In a room filled with 200 people meditating, there is only one common experience going on, but it's happening in 200 different ways. Or, perhaps, in 150 different ways if, as has been my experience with groups learning to meditate, about a quarter of those present are sleeping. Going to sleep is an occupational hazard of meditators—at least for a while. And, believe it or not, that's not matter for guilt, but for amusement.

Meditation is not a mysterious technique you learn to do, but an inner experience you learn to identify. It's learning to recognize *and consciously join* something that's already a real aspect of yourself. It's taking the emphasis off of doing and putting it on consciously *being.* And what does it mean to consciously be? Answering that question is what this book is all about.

———

MEDITATING IS AN INNER UNDERTAKING that is primarily interested in working itself out of a job. It's not made up of discursive thought by which to develop deeper convictions; that kind of inner activity is called study or concentration or even mental prayer. In sharp distinction to such inner discursiveness, meditation is the deliberate search for an experience of what lies beneath all such cerebral busyness. While we do start out using thoughts to gain a new understanding of reality, we do this only in order to recognize the thinker that we are beneath our thoughts. We're seeking an experience of ultimate fulfillment completely beyond thought, of who and what, in our deepest nature, we are.

But what is that grand fulfillment, that profound level of completion, that it is traditionally called bliss? What, exactly, is it that is going to replace all our confusions and fears? It's not a happiness that is object dependent, that results from acquiring, possessing, relating to, or avoiding something. Bliss is based on what we are, not on what we do or own or have done to us. It comes to us when we realize the nature of our innermost life and being, and when we then realize the uncompromised and timeless security and abundance that necessarily accompany that life and being.

————

BUT DOESN'T ALL THIS SEARCH for enlightenment, for bliss, amount to an excessive degree of ego involvement, a simple egocentricity? It may sound that way, but it's actually exactly the opposite. High consciousness is the negation of egocentricity, of egoness of any sort. It means that we have come to see ourselves as a secure, eternally valid, real part of a much greater Whole.

Ego is used in psychology to represent that core of ourselves that we do well to identify, define, and firm up lest we remain fragile and, in effect, filleted. In a spiritual context, however, the word *ego* is used to mean the view of ourselves that is built only on material perceptions and in light of which we see ourselves as small, weak, and alone. Enlightenment is not egocentric because, precisely, it does away with this illusion of our precarious state and substitutes a realization that the real "I," the real "self" of me, is not fragile or weak or in jeopardy in any manner whatsoever. We no longer see ourselves as a small, endangered separateness about which we need to be competitive and, perhaps, defensively aggressive to the point of being dangerously belligerent.

But if this search for enlightenment is not egocentricity, does it not at least foster an indifference to others, a lack of social awareness and sense of race-wide responsibility? Won't the finding of one's own greater self be so self-absorbing an experience that we will no longer feel any need to have concern for others? Again, just the opposite. What I find to be true of me, I find to be equally true of others. After all, everybody is the outpressing of the One; the identically same Existence is in all of us.

———

THE SPIRITUAL PATH—spirituality—means that we pursue an understanding of the nature of reality, our own and God's, and that we then try to channel our thoughts, feelings, and actions accordingly. As understanding grows, we are enticed to close down our outer and, especially, inner franticness long enough to become aware of what we now understand to be our essential life. We want to grasp and experience who we actually are. As this begins to happen, we gain an astonishing sense of security and happiness for which every human being longs. We realize that what we have been seeking is already and necessarily with us as the being of us. Our fulfillment, our bliss, is already here, the essential component of our nature. We've always been in full possession of it. We only needed to learn what to look for, where to look for it, and how to be open to it. *And* where to quit looking.

Jesus knew what he was talking about when he said the kingdom of God is within us. It really is true that we have nothing to gain, only to realize.

As we get the hang of meditation, the contemplative experience begins to happen in us as naturally and irrepressibly as petals unfurling at dawn. It takes some savvy, however, to get to that point. It takes work to stop old ideas and images from getting in the way. Our part of the job is to clarify our thinking so we quit understanding God as a distant—or even present, but separate—artisanlike creator. Least of all as a Supernal Legislator. Our job is to see beyond myth and traditional religious imagery. Our job is to retool our ideas and come to know what it is we are trying to do and the nature of the experience we seek.

———

IF EVERYONE'S INDIVIDUAL SPIRITUAL PROCESS is unique, there is, nonetheless, a common and essential composition to it because the contemplative goal is the same for all. We need to understand what this common denominator is. How, then, does meditation actually work as it leads us to the contemplative experience?

There are three fairly straightforward steps: (1) we read and reflect to understand the ultimate nature of the universe; (2) we strive to retool our thoughts and feelings so they are in line with this new awareness; (3) we make an effort in quiet time to try to experience the full impact of these new understandings. These three steps are our part; the rest is done for us.

You don't have to practice any specific techniques to pursue this path. And, fortunately, you don't have to have a quiet temperament or special talent for concentration. You don't even have to have complete control of your imagination (that's good, because it can't be done anyway). You don't have to sit in a darkened room and light candles or listen to themeless music. You don't have to dedicate a huge swath of time to it or have a certain kind of soft-spoken, unflappable personality. Nor do you have to give up an interest in incarnate things such as delightful food and passionate sex.

All that you must ensure is that, *more than anything else,* you hunger for peace and joy—your ultimate fulfillment.

———

Your unfolding meditative-contemplative process probably will—but need not—flow along the following lines, as it does for many.

1. You begin from wherever you're at. It doesn't matter from how far back you think you're starting. As Anthony of the Desert told scandalized church managers centuries ago when he emerged from a brothel in Alexandria leading a queue of hookers to the desert to transform them into nuns, "I'm like God: I go to get them where they're at." You may be starting out with feelings of self-deprecation, self-rejection, self-doubt, even self-hatred. If you've taken fear-driven, dogmatic religion seriously, you may have a deep sense of being an "awful sinner." You may be tempted to feel that you do not deserve any significant level of bliss. Forget all of that. Move on. The only thing that's of significance now is that you have

decided to undertake a spiritual program. Be glad that you're on your way at last.

2. From wherever your initial experience of meditation begins, if you keep at the practice, you will eventually begin to realize that there is hope on your horizon. You will come to see that you don't have to live life in a self-alienated way any longer. One of the first and most surprising breakthroughs meditators have is the realization that they, too, can achieve bliss.

3. As your meditative efforts continue, you begin to understand that there is another way to view reality than the way you've always taken for granted. You come to understand that your problems—*any* problems—are based on a fear whose foundation is at least questionable and probably quite silly.

4. These first insights usually occur only when you're in your most quiet and self-collected moments. Then, hesitantly, the clarity and reassurance you're starting to feel begin to move out among your daily tasks. You find that you're not so sensitive as before, not so defensive, so rushed or anxious. On many occasions you do still experience your old habits and reactions, of course,

but the point is that more and more often you do not. Remember, meditation is a *process,* and there is no reason for discouragement if you don't change overnight.

5. The coming of a growing peace and reassurance begins to feed your enthusiasm and speed your growth. You find yourself staying more and more in the present moment, with an ever-deepening sense of your oneness with your Source Being.

6. Eventually, breakthrough! You realize—not now because someone else said so, but out of your own convictions and experience—that the mystics and spiritual masters were right. You no longer have to trust others to support your confidence and joy. God is, indeed, with you. You are surrounded by overwhelming love. You are eternally safe. And, in some mysterious way that may not at first be convincing, so is everyone else, despite whatever suffering you see in the world.

———

THE OVERALL PROCESS is that of a person beginning in relative, if not dramatic, confusion and fear and ending in undeniably dramatic clarity, peace, joy, and with a sense of fulfillment. This is the general way that enlightenment comes, regardless of the specifics of from where one started or what practices one used along the way.

The contemplative state belongs to everyone for the taking, not because of the generous condescension of an alleged Divine Legislator, but because that state is nothing more than the unfolding of our deepest nature. Why this is so and how to attain your essential happiness are discussed in the following chapters.

6

IT'S A SPIRITUAL UNIVERSE

You can't ace journalism class until you've aced spelling class. It's no different when you study meditation. You won't be able to follow what's being taught, much less learn to meditate, unless you've learned much about the nature of the universe. It is, for example, both nonmaterial (spiritual) and material, metaphysical and physical. This chapter will explore whether you are convinced in an effectively practical way that the universe is spiritual as well as material, a conviction that is not as common as many people believe.

Largely because religious institutions have squabbled so loudly for centuries and have shamelessly defended contradictory propositions about the nonmaterial dimensions of reality, many people today doubt whether the things of the spirit are objective. Because there is so much disagreement among the self-styled spiritual experts, there is a widespread presumption—as understandable as it is ill-advised—that the best certification for being one's own authority in matters of religion is a birth certificate. Not so. We shouldn't refuse others' assistance in spiritual matters any more than we'd refuse expert help in engineering a bridge. We're foolish if we're wise enough to consult experts for tax planning and health, but think that our own untrained, inexperienced opinions are as informed as anyone's in matters of the spirit. Rejecting help in spiritual matters is a great disservice to oneself, for it closes a person off from information that can be the route into a fulfillment and bliss most people don't even know are waiting for them. And if such skeptics influence others in the process, the loss is compounded.

We all recognize that dentists can fix aching teeth better than can, say, a carpenter. In exactly the same way, it makes sense to recognize that millennia of spiritual writings and the experience and findings of thousands of people who devoted their lives to spirituality know more than newcomers . . . or church managers who are primarily preoccupied with institutional concerns. Students of meditation must be every bit as willing to listen to spiritual experts and get to know and understand the metaphysical side of the universe as they are to listen to other experts when it comes to medicine and finances. We would smile at someone ridiculing Chinese cooking if he admits he's never sampled it. We'd laugh out loud at someone who announces that since he's an auto mechanic he's prepared to explain quantum mechanics to all comers. The need for expertise and experience is no different whatsoever in the realm of spirituality. If we haven't studied deeply, read broadly in spirituality, and meditated successfully, we should be eager to hear what the long spiritual tradition of the human race can teach us.

Why am I making so much of this point? Because it's impossible to learn to meditate without being clear that there is an unseen but most significant dimension to the universe in which we live. To see far in this field, we must, as nowhere else, sit on the shoulders of those who have gone before us.

Learning to Dance Inside

———

IN THIS UNIVERSE there are lots of material things to contact through our bodily senses, like basketballs and golf balls, milk shakes and beer. There are other things that can't be perceived with the senses, but that are equally real: thought and love, honesty and fairness, convictions and hope, for example, and, if you're ready for this, spirits, ascended masters, and an Ultimate Being. Nonmaterial realities are as much a part of the universe as are material objects. They must be neither denied nor ignored simply because they can't be perceived with the bodily senses. The spiritual or metaphysical (words used interchangeably in most contemplative literature) is every bit as real as galaxies and viruses. A feeling of love is just as real as the person loved; the wisdom for living well is just as real as the body in which wisdom will be practiced.

Indeed, spiritual masters tell us that the universe is more a spiritual reality than a material one. If we doubt this bit of data from the spiritual tradition of the human race, we confirm the point I've been making: people dedicated to a lifelong study and practice of spirituality know something about it that the rest of us don't—at least not until we've had the same experience.

There is a great realm of unseen reality that is meant to be part of our wonderment and enjoyment, our growth and fulfillment, our bliss. All of us can be—and by nature are meant to be—as conscious of this spiritual reality as we are of the material aspects of our lives. Spirituality is able to give us a degree of fulfillment and consequent happiness that no material reality can—not money, health, popularity, or the promises and approval of our rabbis, priests, ministers, sheikhs, shamans, roshis, gurus, or devoutly pious relatives.

———

UNFORTUNATELY, THE WORD *spiritual* has been largely taken over by religious institutions and given a meaning—or at least a connotation—that is different from its real meaning. Institutionalized religions often use spiritual for any of the material things with which they are preoccupied. For most of them the word means religion-related, if not actually institution-related. They use it to identify their concern for institutional conformity and perpetuation, for approved propriety and practice, for daily logistics of keeping large edifices afloat, and even for Sunday collections—"your spiritual offerings." Organized religion employs the word freely and, more often than not, wrongly, all the while presuming ownership of it.

The truth is that institutionalized religion has little or no actual *spiritual* knowledge or expertise simply because it has for so long been more concerned with external conformity, propriety, logistics, and self-perpetuation than with things of the Spirit.

Students of meditation must realize that the word *spiritual,* instead, refers to the nonmaterial dimension of the universe. This distinction becomes doubly important when many people who have rejected the external practice of religion feel that, to be consistent, they must also reject whatever is said to be spiritual. They are unwittingly buying organized religion's presumed ownership of the term, and so they throw out the one with the other. They haven't stopped to remember that the practice of spirituality long predates religious institutions.

You don't have to give any kind of nod whatsoever to a religious organization in order to reclaim the spiritual in your life.

7

RETOOLING RELIGIOUS IDEAS

If a factory that makes buggy whips wants to start producing auto parts, it has to retool by installing new machines. If you've been a monk forever and eventually decide you want an intimate companion in life, you'd better get over your concern about being close to women or you'll limit your options considerably. (I know whereof I speak; I only managed to get comfortable around women at the age of forty.) Both cases illustrate the point that outdated resources, outer or inner, won't work for achieving updated goals.

In exactly the same way, if we want to quit manufacturing inner uncertainty, fear, and psychological guilt, we need to upgrade or replace the ideas and images out of which these distresses are being created. Our old resources obviously haven't worked for our peace, so we have a right (and duty) to decide to try some new ones. We need to acquire new insights and understandings, ones that will be more effective in serving our fulfillment. If buggy whips don't make your vehicle move, try installing a motor.

———

RETOOLING OUR IDEAS and images of God doesn't mean we have to throw out whatever religion we already have. But it very well may mean—and usually does—that we must update what we have by searching for its inner content and by no longer being satisfied to understand its stories literally. When people with no religion begin to meditate, they sometimes move along more quickly than churchgoers because they don't have to spend so much time retooling their God-related images and ideas. They don't have to struggle through religious stories and images that have been understood literally since childhood.

Change shouldn't frighten us. Life is a process,

part of which goes on whether we like it or not, whether we knowingly participate in it or not. Our bodies, for example, grew from infancy into adulthood, and society's expectations of us grew more exacting as we aged—whether we were prepared for this added responsibility or not. Other parts of our process, on the other hand, require our explicit attention and deliberate effort. If we don't work at it, for example, our minds will remain infantile and uninformed. That most independent thinker and unlikely Roman cardinal, John Henry Newman, put this process of human unfolding into perspective when he wrote, "To be perfect is to have changed often."

MANY PEOPLE—including, undoubtedly, most who are reading this book—are ready to reassess their ideas and images and retool them as needed. Most people today are ready for the higher things in life, the "more," of which spiritual masters spoke. They are ready to believe something more critical, more informed, than the doctrine and view of the earth as God's divine boot camp. They know they aren't children any longer and must not leave their understanding at the level of ancient childhood stories. The race is no longer infantile.

We will have to do better than thinking of God as some sort of superpowerful, potentially dangerous, patriarchlike Ruler somewhere out there in the cosmos if we hope to learn to meditate and come to the joy and freedom of mature enlightenment. Even tacking on the assurance that the traditional patriarch-ruler God is forgiving and somehow lovingly present to us still leaves us with a separate Being. At least according to the mystics and spiritual masters who shared with us their insights and experiences, any notion of separateness is the stuff of story. Whether it's the ancient Egyptian Plotinus or the modern Hindu Ramana Maharshi, the Hasidic Ba'al Shem Tov, the Taoist Lao-tzu, the Christian Meister Eckhart, or the ex-Christian Alan Watts, all things are seen as being one with the Eternal Being—exactly, for example, as the master teacher Jesus, within the Judeo-Christian tradition, said about all of us and "the Father" being one. We are invited to get beneath all stories and other variables within diverse religious cultures that represent God as separate and find their inner content and meaning. We are invited to seek a degree of inner realization that will set us free and start our hearts dancing.

Santa Claus is a fictional figure we present to young children as their first lesson in the rewards of good living. It works for them, but who of us, as adults, would want only this fictional character on which to base our commitment to generous giving and good living? Fortunately, unlike Santa, God is real, even though the stories about Him are fictional teaching accounts no more literal than the story of Santa Claus. It takes more than the stuff of stories to acquire a substantial and liberating experience of God. We will not be adequately convinced or committed to seek enlightenment and bliss if all we have as the basis of our search and ultimate inner reality is the Bible and its Santa-level stories about God.

As long as we think of the universe as a place where we are being tested on how obediently we keep a set of divinely imposed rules, the best meditation we will ever know will be a kind of mental prayer that muses on God's alleged requirements and then, possibly, finds joy in the happy confidence that we are meeting them, or, in the case of Christians, that Jesus has kept them for us. That may be a reassuring and pleasant experience, but it's certainly not an enlightenment giving birth to bliss. It amounts to no more than the imagined assurance of a judge's nod of approval.

The notion of there being a king in the sky with a long list of laws was first told to a young race to get it started on the road to reaching for more in the universe than other people's possessions. Seeing God as a benevolent, loving ruler is not a bad start, and such an image is still useful for launching many into wanting to know more about God. Some individuals may have to stay with this impression of God for an extended period, just as some need the threat of sanctions even as adults to keep them from a life of crime. Many people, however, manage to avoid crime without the need for threats. As the human race continues to accelerate its understanding, increasing numbers are no longer helped by the lingering image of a kinglike God passed down from an age of kings.

IF YOU WANT TO FEEL CLOSER to the inner reality of the universe, to understand it better, feel safer and happier in it, you're ready to start meditating seriously. If you want to respect and love yourself, others, and the world about you—and if you want to jettison all guilt about the past, about your imagined inadequacy, and all anxiety about your future, you're ready. It doesn't matter, at this stage, how little you know about meditation or how foreign or even airy it may seem. *All you really need to begin with is a resolution to work for adult understanding.* This is not a difficult task, but it's an essential one.

An otherwise bright and accomplished woman confided to me once that she had checked with her church authorities and was warned that "Prayer comes from God, but meditation from Satan." This rather astonishing guidance and patent ignorance are timely reminders for all of us to inventory what sort of attitudes may be quietly holed up in our thoughts and feelings. If any of these attitudes are foolish, no matter where we got them, we become just as foolish as they are if we let them influence us. We do well to audit our presuppositions and beliefs rather frequently. What other than unrecognized fear could have made my well-intentioned informant accept, without uproarious laughter, the pronouncement from her church leaders that meditation comes from the devil? Their counsel has an all-too-obvious underpinning of fear. They know well that meditation frees people from dependence on outside religious authority. Many church leaders, more concerned for institutional growth than for the fulfillment of their flock, are totally consistent in advising against meditation.

If you're attracted to meditation, but find you're vaguely reluctant to pursue it—as many are, even while they read books about it—ask yourself why. Could it be that somewhere deep inside you fear you may be constrained to alter beliefs you have been taught by some important ecclesiastical authority? Do you fear you may be pressed to re-examine what daddy or grandma or a respected pastor taught you or what your family has believed for generations? Could it be that you are being controlled by the warning you once received that you'd better stick to familiar teaching or you may go to hell?

Most of organized religion is still faithful to the practices of an era that demanded unquestioning submission from adherents. Some people fear spiritual independence for no more substantial reason than that they grew up in the West where much of the thinking about God is still a holdover from an extravagantly credulous period of history. There are areas in the West where "faith" is still preached exactly as it was when ignorance, superstition, and regional bias were as common as education, individual creativity, and global exchange of information are today.

———

REGARDLESS OF WHERE your basic spiritual presuppositions come from, alert your conscious mind to all of them. I'm not suggesting that you give up your beliefs, and I'm certainly not prescribing new beliefs. I am, however, openly telling you that if you want to grow, to meditate, to find your bliss, you will usually have to reassess your beliefs—and probably, as a consequence, also have to deepen them. I'm inviting you to search for knowable reality yourself and to form your own conclusions. Since I'm not telling you what those conclusions should be, I'm not pushing a new dogmatism. If in this book I write confidently about what the general parameters of your conclusions will most likely be, it's not because they must be so, but because of my knowledge of the historical evidence of how spiritual growth and insight have developed around the globe, as well as of how it has developed for myself and for the many individuals with whom I've worked.

If, in your reassessment of your familiar beliefs, you discover that you still believe what others taught you only because they taught them to you, your good sense will suggest that you look at these beliefs more critically. You may end up not getting rid of any of them, or you may dump most of them. But at very least, you will make what you believe your own. You alone will then be responsible for whether your convictions help or hinder your search for human fulfillment, for bliss.

Even our most closely held inner convictions—about religion, politics, family, race—must always be evolving, and therefore deepening. Otherwise, we're like a rosebud that's so pleased with itself as a bud that it refuses to move on to become a complete blossom.

From the time we were little children, society pushed us to grow. In math, for example, we were moved along so we could one day handle our finances; in self-determination, so we could one day vote intelligently; in personal responsibility, so we would be prepared to take on the challenges of a job and of raising a family. In religion alone are vast numbers of people urged *not* to grow. They are routinely advised (and not infrequently threatened) to leave their faith exactly where it was when they first heard it as children from a catechism, a religious school, or at mama's knee. Those who choose to do differently, and to critique what it is they believe, have long been called heretics, a word that from its Greek root means those who make their own choice. In previous eras, such freedom was roundly condemned, and this infantile notion lingers in many places even today.

Learning to Dance Inside

When given a chance through study and encouragement, our spiritual understanding (a more adequate word for adult belief than the word *faith*) will automatically develop into deeper, higher, and more critically informed levels. If we are discouraged from developing these qualities—and if we pay attention to such abusive guidance—our understanding of religion and life in its higher reaches will stagnate. It's not surprising that many adults feel confused, unfulfilled, and unhappy when they don't bother to critique and monitor their inner beliefs. Without an adult level of spiritual fulfillment, adults *should* feel confused and unhappy: the greater part of themselves is stagnant and suppressed.

If there is even a remote chance you subtly suspect that meditation will compromise your religion or that God is some kind of note-taking monarch—or that your eternal security in any manner depends on blind adherence to ancient formulas, your challenge is to open your mind and allow for other possibilities. Many have been convinced by vested or timid interests—by family, congregational, or other expectations, for example—to delay any hope for real fulfillment until "the next life." As long as individuals are convinced they must forfeit this life for the sake of the next, nothing can be done in the way of either highest spiritual growth or genuine fulfillment here in this one. This is a choice each of us must make.

———

MEDITATION WILL HELP THOSE who want to be helped. If you are one of these, it will help you expand into a new, deeper, more personal relationship with yourself, with all around you, with the world, *and* with that Ultimate Reality of the universe most call God.

All of us, of any persuasion, need to check to see if we are free to follow the invitation from within to activate our potential and to move into a new and vigorous spiritual vitality. The Spanish mystics of sixteenth-century Spain had to weigh their spiritual insights carefully against the organizational norms set by the Inquisition, and many were careless and ended up on the rack or tied to a stake surrounded by kindling. Unlike them, we are in no physical danger. We have that sort of repressive monitoring in our lives today only as long as we permit it.

———

As soon as we begin to realize the results of meditation, as soon as the *experience* of the deepest and highest realities in the universe begin to be ours, we no longer have the slightest doubt that our effort—our "risk," if you feel constrained to think of it that way—was worthwhile.

8

BEYOND RELIGIOUS STORIES

Sometimes in order to understand something new, we have to compare it with something that we already understand. Tell me that someone I'm thinking of doing business with is a weasel, and I get your point immediately. Tell me my speech was a bomb, and you don't have to elaborate. Usually the intangible, spiritual elements in our reality, the invisible parts of it, have to be learned with the help of comparisons with and stories about material things. That's why spiritual teachers throughout history have made up stories or created myths with which to pass their spiritual insights and realizations along to others.

Think of how we teach values and principles of right living to small children. We don't talk to them in abstract terms about goodness or honor or the ethical rules of fair play and community responsibility. We weave simple guidelines into stories about good and shining fairies and about ugly, wicked goblins. Stories and imagery get ideas across to children much better than abstract discussions ever could.

The same procedure has been used throughout history to teach values and spiritual principles to adults. There have always been people who wanted to share their spiritual breakthroughs and who found that storytelling is the best—and often the only—way to do this. For as far back as we can trace, teachers and spiritual masters have composed myths and used fairy tales, poetry, comparisons, and exaggerated epic history to get a point across. They had to depend on this way of teaching in a day when few would have understood or believed or remembered what they said otherwise. Even today we may not understand spiritual realities without learning aids.

———

ANCIENT SPIRITUAL TEACHERS told stories about magic trees, about a divinely powerful moon, about sacred animals, hugely exaggerated military victories, angels with wings like soaring eagles. The God they met in their best contemplative moments was so beyond description that they compared their experience to meeting a supremely venerable grandfather, the sun, a mighty river, a great king. In patriarchies such as the Hebrew tradition, God was seen as male; in matriarchies and in cultures where the female element was well recognized, God was painted as a venerable woman or Great Mother. Except for the accident of history that Judaism happened to be a patriarchy, Christians today might find themselves praying, "Our Mother, who art in heaven. . . ."

———

BUT HOW DO WE KNOW that spiritual teachers actually did have higher experiences for which they composed myths and stories and thought up comparisons? In any individual case, we don't. Nevertheless, in the observed overall development of religion, we can see a trend from simple tales to deeper meaning, from myth to understanding of myth, from hearing stories to grasping their content. For example, Jesus told parables and then later explained their inner meaning (as in Luke 8:11, for those who are interested in Christian Testament references). It is not a stretch of logic to conclude that if tales have deeper meanings, at least most of their authors had those meanings in mind when they composed them.

Sometimes the originators of religious myths and storyforms wove actual realities and incidents into their telling, but because their point was religious teaching, the stories do not teach history, geography, astronomy, physics, or other nonreligious topics. The Santa Claus tale has several important messages for children, but none of them are about the ability of reindeer to pull sleds through the sky or of fat men to fit inside chimneys. Similarly, the two creation stories in the book of Genesis are not intended to teach that God is literally an artisan creating a universe in six working days, making humankind by fashioning a mud doll, poofing life into it, and then stopping for a beer on the seventh. The challenge for students who read religious stories and myths is to realize that they are not meant to be taken literally. They are just stepping-stones to the deeper, intangible, nonmaterial messages they contain. At whatever level of awareness religious storyforms are created, their creators—modern as well as ancient—share what they can and trust that the listeners will, in good time, understand what is behind their telling.

———

AN OBVIOUS PROBLEM easily arises. Children sometimes panic at the thought of giving up their belief in the literal truth of a tale in which they have invested much emotion. "Santa just has to be real!" they wail as the awful truth is presented to them for the first time by a more precocious playmate. In exactly the same way—and wailing just as loudly—some adults panic when it is suggested that their Bible stories are only storyforms. They are as reluctant to move beyond the literalness of their Bible as children are to give up Santa Claus, only instead of limiting their reaction to wailing, adults often go on to react with threats, hatred, pogroms, crusades, inquisitions, threats of damnation. This is not too surprising when we realize that some biblical stories have threats about not being taken literally built right into them. The last verses of the final book of the Bible, for example, have terrified Christians into unquestioning submission for centuries. Fear is the powerful mother of all irrational persuasions.

The difficulty of accepting change can be especially marked when a set of religious stories stands alone in a person's bank of knowledge, and similar stories from other cultures remain unknown. This impoverishment means that honest seekers of truth are not given the opportunity to compare, evaluate, and sort as they try to move from the details of a story to its substance and content. We can learn the basic, innermost meaning of our own culture's great religious stories more easily if we become familiar with those of other cultures.

———

Beyond Religious Stories

AN ADDITIONAL PROBLEM in reinterpreting myths and stories is that change itself, in the best of cases, is not comfortable for many people. Some find it difficult to undertake almost anything that involves leaving the familiar for the unfamiliar, even if it's a matter of leaving a tumbled-down shack to move into a commodious new house down the block. How much more reluctant will such people be when asked to reinterpret religious stories that have dominated their minds and feelings, unchallenged and unchanged, all their lives.

It's human, it's understandable, and it's perfectly healthy to cry at school graduation. But if the confusion and emotions behind our tears induce us not to leave school, we have a problem. Anyone who surveys the religious scene objectively will see that the problem of people being unwilling to graduate from childhood's religious stories is widespread. Organized religion, as a whole, has almost never encouraged people to graduate from simple observance, conformity, and uncritical, literal acceptance of myths. With few exceptions, religious institutions have taught that religion is a closed system of static observance and noncreative conformity. It hardly ever encourages unlimited growth and open-ended insight.

Meditation is the path out of this morass of infantilism. It's a ready way to see and experience just how grand and extensive the human circumstance is.

9

THE UNDERLYING FACT

What, then, lies within, beneath, and beyond all myth and religious storyforms? The answer is simple once it's understood, but it's often difficult to grasp at first.

This is the only chapter in this book that may cause headaches. And it'll do that only if you let it. A television commercial some years ago had the jingle, "Try it; you'll like it." Perhaps the jingle here should be: "Try it; you may not like it, but you need it anyway."

———

WHATEVER ELSE CAN BE SAID about the ultimate spiritual nature of the universe, it's still true that for the practical purpose of living in this world, the material feet of our material bodies stand on material ground. Regardless of how spiritual I believe the universe to be, if I fall off a cliff, an uncompromisingly material pile of completely inflexible rocks will greet me at the bottom. And yet spiritual masters tell us that as our inner awareness of universal reality grows, we will see that even the material aspects of the universe, even the rocks at the bottom of a cliff, are expressions of—outpressings of—the spiritual. That doesn't make the material world less real to deal with; it only explains its source and inner nature. Rocks don't have reflective consciousness, it's true, but they do have the same being, the same source existence, that intelligent beings have.

Human reason and good sense will assure anyone who thinks about it that there is a common element underlying everything that exists. Even if there are uncounted numbers of universes, everything in every one of them has one quality in common: it exists. Each thing—no matter how or where or when—has an identical and common, ultimate, innermost reality to it that we call "existence." No matter where or how it shows up, existence is existence is existence. It's always exactly the same thing—always the is-ness of whatever is.

Existence is simply *be*-ing, not how or where something is, but simply *that* it is. Whether as the biggest rock somewhere in the Andromeda galaxy or as the smallest bit of pollen clinging to a honeybee on earth, existence is present or the rock and pollen would not be there.

Existence itself doesn't differ in any way no matter where it is because only *after* something exists, only after it *is*, does it become something big or green or thin or spiritual or material. Existence is identically the same in everything; differences can show up in things only when and if and after they *are*—only, that is, after they have the basic, common, identical quality called existence. (Need to read that one more time? It's important, and if you stop to think carefully about it, it's not difficult to grasp.)

Other than in everyday conversation, something either is or. . . we can't even say that "it is not," because if it doesn't exist, there is no "it" to discuss. There are *not* two possibilities for an "it": a thing either is, or there is nothing there to make a statement about.

All the "somethings" in all universes have existence in common because they all exist, no matter how differently they do it. Apart from *how* they express, there isn't any difference between this be-ing and that be-ing; that is to say, apart from things existing as big or green or soft or fast, the only difference possible is between being and not-being, thing and no-thing. Whether something is as big as a universe or as small as a quark, as material as a mountain or as immaterial as a thought, there is the one, single, identical characteristic common to everything that is: existence. Otherwise, there would be no things to talk about because they would not exist.

Moreover, this common existence can't be divided. It can exist here or there, now or later, but in itself it always simply *is*. The manner in which something exists is distinct from the more immediate fact *that* it exists. And existence is nothing more than the identical "isness" of everything that is. There can't be one kind of existence here and another kind over there, one kind today and another kind tomorrow. That would be to see it as an infinite daub of clay that can be divided into smaller daubs. Being, existence, is not a daub of anything. It is the isness, the being, of all daubs, so to speak.

———

YOU MAY BE WONDERING what all this has to do with meditation. It has everything to do with it, but before explaining why, it's necessary to digress to make a disclaimer.

There is a huge difference between the dogmatism of individual cultures and opposing religions and the unqualified statements, like the above, of metaphysics. There is a difference between what global human reason itself has come to realize and what individual cultures and subcultures realize in their distinctive circumstances. It's one thing for a segment of the world's population to claim it has an option on truth, but it's quite another for human reason itself, and as a whole, to take itself as valid. Specific doctrines are one thing; what the deepest philosophical thinking of the human race as a whole has discovered and generally agreed upon is another.

This is not to say that when discussing the nature of existence, everyone everywhere will agree on all points. But it is to recognize that the metaphysical insight of worldwide thoughtfulness and spirituality is in general agreement, because when human reason and the human spirit investigate reality—considered apart from where local and vested interests come into play—the core conclusions are, not surprisingly, consistent. It's only when the discussion moves further, and this or that region of the world claims special, self-righteous, superior advantages for its thought and cultural bias, that dogmatism in the pejorative sense enters the picture. Only then do narrowness and bigotry and conflict appear. It is not, then, inconsistent for this book to decry, as it does, the dogmatism of individual religions and yet speak confidently in some detail about the underlying agreement on ultimate metaphysics common to spiritual masters everywhere. The conflicts have to do with pet doctrines and externals; the agreement comes from what is spiritual, metaphysical.

The Underlying Fact

———

ANY DISCUSSION OF METAPHYSICS, of the existence that underlies all things, will at first seem opaque and will, by its nature, stretch our thinking. When talking about meditation and the contemplative experience, however, it's necessary to pursue these discussions, howsoever obscure, because spiritual masters have shared a fundamental realization with us that makes all this talk about existence affect meditation. When we talk about existence and *being* as we did in the above paragraphs, it's probably inevitable at first to imagine a vague, abstract, mindless, indifferent quality that is somehow at the heart of all reality. What spiritual masters report, however—and what we will eventually experience for ourselves—is that this existence is not indifferent or vague or impersonal. And certainly it's not at all abstract or mindless. The ultimate, most central, deepest part of all of us, of everything—the reality that we call being—is precisely the same underlying reality, source, as that which various cultures, including the Judeo-Christian tradition, have called Creator and God. Suddenly we are no longer talking about an impersonal, vague sort of underlying abstraction most people think of when they think of existence, but about Existence with a capital *E*. We speak now of Ultimate Being, not just of being; of Life, not of just lowercase life. If God *is* existence, then the conventions of our language demand that the word Existence be capitalized and, in fact, be understood as another word for the Source Being, for what most people call God.

When I say in this book, then, that God is Existence, I am not in any way suggesting that God is an abstract and impersonal isness underlying all things. I am summarizing a transcultural spiritual insight and tradition that teaches exactly the opposite. The mystics of the world do not experience and then teach that a vague and impersonal existence is the Source Being. Rather, they share their realization of the Source Being as the Eternal Being that outpresses all things as expressions of Itself. In the cultural expression used by Jesus, for example, everything is "One with the Father." Every ray of the sun shares the life of the sun, but, for all that, the sun remains central and foundational and their source. The sunrays together do not make up the sun, and, yet, each of them is an immediate outpressing of it, and it is forever their being, the existence of each of them.

Most of us tend to look at reality from the wrong end. We see many apparently separate things and then conclude that all of these have been made by a supreme artisan. Contemplative spirituality invites us to look at our surrounding universe differently, as the mystics do. See Being first, and *then* see all other things as the expressions of (the outpressings of) that Source Being. All that exists can only exist by sharing the only Existence there is.

———

ANOTHER CONSIDERATION is necessary. God doesn't have Existence; God *is* Existence. Logic shows that God either *is* the existence spoken of above or had to receive it from another. If the one we call God only *has* existence, then that existence was already possessed by that other who, thus, predates God and so becomes itself the ultimate Source of life and being and must itself be called Ultimate Reality,

God. In either case, however, we see that there is an Ultimate Being who *is* Existence. And that One is customarily called God. Again: God doesn't have Existence; God *is* Existence.

———

IT'S HAZARDOUS TO USE THE WORD *God* in serious exchange because most people in the West understand it to signify an elderly monarch and master artisan of the cosmos who seems terribly concerned about getting his daily ration of recognition (cryptically called glory). As the storyform paints him, God seems to be a demanding and not very likable schoolteacher with one helluva punishment up his sleeve for nonperformers. Religious leaders keep dutifully repeating that he's somehow loving anyway, but it's difficult to buy their juxtaposition of love and eternal fire. Like most other storyforms, this one, too, can't bear close scrutiny.

I recognize the usefulness for religious teachers to refer to a patriarchal divinity somewhere off in the cosmos or somehow inside of us when instructing children and spiritual beginners. It is paramount always to remember, however, that they are only telling a story, albeit a story with an important content. Anyone wishing to move along to the contemplative experience of God—anyone, that is, wishing to meditate—must move beyond this story and concentrate on its content, the Eternal Reality that lies within it.

———

THE WORD *God*, as used in most cultures of the West, certainly does not accurately represent the sort of Ultimate Source Being about which spiritual masters tell us. They are masters of spirituality precisely because they don't confuse religious stories with the spiritual content of those stories. They teach that the basic, one Existence which all things—including us—have in common is a sharing of the Source Itself, of the Per-Se Existence, of the Life that is the innermost Nature of Reality.

As mentioned before, this is not pantheism because it's not saying that God is made up of all things. Things didn't come first, with God thereby resulting. Sunrays together don't make up the sun even though they all outpress from it and share its being. Eternal Being *is,* and all that exists about us flows from It and is one with It. We are each simply one facet, one expression of the sole Existence there is. As Hindu theology puts it, "You are That." You and I are distinct individuals, yes, but we are not separate in our innermost Nature—just as the facets of a gem reflect light individually, but forever remain part of the same jewel.

———

THE EXISTENCE ALL OF US share exists forever. To be more accurate, Existence is eternal, and eternity is, in the words of the ancient Roman philosopher Boethius, "the total *and simultaneous* possession of all life." "Forever" is merely a way we humans have of identifying the aspect of timelessness in the Source Being. God just *Is,* with no sequence in Its continuing. In order to understand this idea more easily, we think of eternity and timelessness as an endlessly ongoing sequence of nows, and then we call that sequence forever. In point of fact, there is no such sequence whatsoever in eternity and timelessness.

A related consideration is not immediately apparent, either. The Source Being, again by Its very Nature, not only always is, but it could never not Be. Think about it: the statement contains a contradiction in terms. It's contradiction to say that a person can stand and sit at the same time. Similarly, to say that existence cannot exist, that being cannot be, is a contradiction.

————

THE SOURCE BEING EXPRESSES ITSELF, outpresses its Being, as all things, and we see the result as what we call creation. The Judeo-Christian creation myth in the Bible—essentially matching the many creation tales of other cultures—tells of a Divine Artisan making all things out of nothing. The biblical Genesis story of creation is the West's primary storyform, but despite its literal reading, Eternal Being didn't reach into nothingness and "create" things; It simply outpressed expressions of Its own

Existence from the field of infinite possibilities that Being, by its very Nature, is. Or, as some modern physicists like to put it, "The possible is brought into actuality out of an infinite probability amplitude." The idea being talked about is more available to most of us when we simply state that Eternal Being delights Itself by outpressing in countless varieties of forms.

———

PEOPLE WHO HAVE BEEN RAISED in the Judeo-Christian culture may feel uneasy that their biblical writings do not speak explicitly of Existence or of much that is written here. (People who are helped by biblical references should note that the name the Source Being gave itself in the Torah, Yahweh, is a derivative of the Hebrew verb *to be.* Scholars argue about the exact translation of the four Hebrew letters making up this name, but they do agree that it makes some sort of reference to being a cause, source, or something related.) We need to remember that a metaphysical explanation of God as the origin of all things would not have been comprehensible to most people in the era when the creation myths of the world were composed. Religious myths were created to stand in for deeper understandings to come later. Paul of Tarsus, the most prolific and arguably most sophisticated writer in the Christian Testament, confesses in his second letter to the Corinthians (12:2) that he has heard things in meditation that "man is not permitted to speak"—realizations that were, that is, so far beyond his contemporaries' points of reference and understanding that they were better left unsaid. Jesus, too, said there were higher understandings to be realized at a later time when, in John's account of his life, he told his listeners that he had "much more to say to you, more than you can now bear." (John 16:12) Implying that there would be a later time when such understanding would be possible, he went on in the same conversation to promise, that "when the Spirit comes, he will lead you into all [this additional] truth"—when, that is, human growth has finally learned to respond to inside prompting and no longer feels constrained to parrot and conform to the socially familiar.

Learning to Dance Inside

——

THE SOURCE BEING exists *as* all things and is "in" them only in that sense. All things do not live *in* It, and It does not live *in* them; It lives *as* them.

But why talk about "them"? The point of this book is to help you learn *and experience* that all of the above applies to *you*. Eternal Being expresses Its Being as *you!*

Meditation is the effort to experience this fact. Contemplative bliss is the experiencing of it.

10

A NEW WAY OF FINDING GOD

The idea that God is a totally separate entity is deeply ingrained in most of the West. Christian churches simply don't know how to handle in any practical manner the underlying doctrine and contemplative realization of the oneness of God and all things. To their confusion—but fortunately for the cause of spiritual growth—their own Testament more than once talks about this Oneness. In Acts 17:28, for example, it says "in him we live and move and have our being." Jesus himself said the same thing in so many words (John 17:21): "that all of them may be one, Father, just as you are in me, and I in you. . . ." This realization appears even more often and explicitly in the Christian Gnostic gospels recovered at Nag-Hammadi in the desert of Upper Egypt. Some church traditions leave the whole idea of the oneness of God and "creation" strictly alone. Others have developed elaborate and arcane teachings around it, the unnecessarily obfuscated doctrine of the Mystical Body of Christ in Roman Catholicism being but the most striking example.

In the East, on the contrary, dominant spiritual traditions explicitly prepare adherents for the practical consequence of realizing the underlying oneness of all things. Hinduism, for example, urges spiritual aspirants to long for the full realization of their oneness with Eternal Being. Buddhism and Taoism never said we were separate in the first place. Prepared or not, in East or West, insofar as one begins to realize union with God, a change is required in how one prays or is in any manner accustomed to deal with a supposedly separate Source Being.

Insofar as we have been trained to think of prayer as dialogue, even if at times a wordless dialogue, it's always an exchange of some sort between two separate individuals, God and the one praying. This give-and-take easily becomes the central joy of a spiritually inclined person's life. Contact with God becomes so familiar and intimate and delightfully reassuring that it's like having a special confidant beside one every moment of every day. God becomes so real and talking with Him so special that there is not even a remote suspicion that this inner intimacy could ever disappear.

What happens to such familiar inner habits, however, when there is no longer a separate God in the scheme of things? Does the "Our Father" become obsolete for Christians, for example? And even for those who do not pray, how do they think about a God who is no longer understood as distinct from their own being? Union with God may seem a mere academic possibility at first, but questions about its implications become practical—and then pressing—as meditation moves one into a growing awareness and experience of oneness. Philosophical explanations that may have seemed reasonable before suddenly seem inadequate. It's not uncommon for an advancing meditator to cry out at such times, partly in dismay, largely in panic, "I've lost my God! I used to get so much comfort from talking intimately with God, but now . . .

how am I supposed to be praying now? To whom do I turn now?"

Ultimately, because the process of spiritual development is not haphazard or without purpose, all confusion will clear up. Such an assurance about the future provides little comfort, however, to those in the throes of a dramatic apparent loss.

There is no getting around the fact that customary prayer and patterns of thought have to change. Until that happens, and in so far as people remain inflexibly committed to understanding God as a separate being, they know panic. I did. But as quickly as we understand that this evolution of inner realization is a breakthrough into a deeper awareness of and closeness to God, we find ourselves—after only brief confusion—experiencing an intimacy multiplied many times beyond what we previously knew.

A charmingly simple, young Carmelite nun, now deceased, Sister Elizabeth of the Trinity, described the mounting confusion she felt as her mysticism unfolded. In light of her Christian orthodoxy, the best she could manage was, "I feel dwelt in." She had moved beyond traditional piety to what Christian mystic tradition calls mystical union. Teresa of Avila and John of the Cross had the same experience, and it's interesting to watch them try to write about it while knowing that the Spanish inquisitors, with their store of racks, fire, and holy thumbscrews, would be the first to read every word. The Roman church has always held mystical union in high regard, at least theoretically and, of course, only as long as it remained subject to the superior wisdom of the ruling powers in Rome. This held true whether or not those powers had time for, experience of, or interest in personal spirituality themselves.

——

WHAT DOES COMMERCE with the Source Being look like after the coming of higher consciousness and contemplative union? A comparison is helpful.

It's a fairly basic spiritual realization that God is neither masculine nor feminine, and yet, because of the limits of human language, we still must use some sort of personal pronoun if we are going to talk in a not-too-convoluted way about Ultimate

Reality. It's simply too confusing, for example, to refer to God as He/She/It to avoid gender implications. The most practical tactic is to face the fact that language breaks down when we talk about One who has no gender and is yet not neuter. As a conscious compromise, common usage suggests that we simply continue to refer to God as He despite the recognized risk that some listeners may suspect a male chauvinism lurking in our bushes. (Another way, of course, is to refer to the Supreme Being as She and really keep people loose.)

This problem of divine pronouns is similar to what we face when we want to speak to God after we've realized that our Source and we are one. We may find that we only know how to address Him as though separate, if we want to communicate in a meaningful way. The dilemma is only apparent. Our dialogue may continue as before, the difference being that now we know it's a compromise, built on a fiction of separateness and required not by the nature of things, but by the limits of our language. Thus, Jesus himself could say that he and God are one, and that whoever sees him (Jesus) sees the Father and yet, in the same conversation, talk to God as if separate and address Him as Father (John, chapters 14-17). Father remains a usable form of address for any degree of intimacy with an Ultimate Source who is thus the pattern of all begetting. The word is not wrong; it's simply inadequate. It will have to do, however, until contemplative experience takes us beyond words.

———

HOWEVER SUBLIME it may be, inner dialogue will eventually be submerged in conscious inner union, a condition infinitely more sublime than the expression of intimacies characteristic of the close separateness this union has displaced. Inner dialogue gives way to inner dance, to unimaginable joy that often expresses itself—as the lives of many contemplatives illustrate—in a spiritual outrageousness and freedom that shocks those who still think of religion in terms of conformity, propriety, and juridical obligation.

When Jesus said, "The Father and I are One" and "Before Abraham was, I Am," some of his pious listeners were convinced he spoke blasphemy and were supremely outraged—outraged enough to have him put to death for it. And yet the mystical tradition of both West and East—more cautiously and more rarely in the West—proclaims that he was exactly accurate. Even though Christian churches have manipulated these statements of Jesus for centuries to make them fit their separate-God dogma, the power of the contemplative experience that comes to those who seek it convinces them in an instant that the teachings about a separate God are simply in error and that Jesus, unedited, was right.

After the thirteenth-century scholar and ranking theologian Thomas Aquinas had attained the contemplative experience—a man who had written millions of words in tightly reasoned defense of Christian doctrines—he stopped his writing and would write no more. When his Dominican prior pressed him to continue, he quietly said that what he had now been shown in meditation made all that he had previously written to be "only straw." A tradition has it that he wrote no more for the remainder of his life.

———

BECAUSE THE PROCESS of experiencing the ramifications of contemplative union is gradual, one should not prematurely drop, much less feel obligated to drop, the dialogue of prayer. A meditator should move away from outer or inner dialogue only when it becomes an inner imperative and feels like the most simple, natural, consistent, necessary expedient in the world.

In the end, the cessation of conversational prayer is not the loss—or, as some see it, the blasphemy—that customary thinking fears. To apply the biblical metaphor often used for God's intimacy with humans: If I marry the girl down the block and am making love to her in our own bed, it's foolish to long for previous times when I held her hands on her parents' front porch. We still hold hands, indeed, but now there is so much more. Prayer as dialogue is a *beginning* form of communion. But now there is union.

No schedule. No threats. No danger. And no urgency . . . unless you're anxious to know divine intimacy.

11

TWO CLARIFICATIONS

The spiritual life is never complicated, but it may and usually does seem so in its earlier stages. Ask almost anyone who has meditated for years, and as likely as not you'll be regaled with tales of intemperate early efforts and passionate panic in ways and degrees that were later recognized as both unnecessary and humorous.

While owning initial extravagances, however, an experienced meditator will almost always be eager also to share special insights and lessons learned so that others will not make the same mistakes and go off on unnecessary detours.

To continue the discussion of the last chapter and to broaden its scope, I will add two particularly significant clarifications in this chapter that I once found more than usually helpful and that individuals with whom I've worked have subsequently reported they found helpful as well.

———

THE FIRST INSIGHT is a reminder that while meditation for many must start with an upgrading of religious images, ideas, and explicit understanding, even this essential reasoning will eventually give way to nonconceptual silence. The stress that this book puts on retooling concepts and deepening understanding does not contravene the ultimate disappearance of conceptualization and discursiveness for the sake of the (nonconceptual) contemplative experience.

The apparent inconsistency of using reason to transcend reason can be better understood if we appreciate the difference between the paths of those led primarily by their hearts and those led by their minds. The way of the heart and the way of the mind both end up in nonconceptual silence and bliss, but the two routes to this common point differ substantially. These two ways have appeared in various spiritual cultures under different guises: sometimes explicitly identified and named in a given religious culture, sometimes only obvious from an analysis of the variations within a culture's spiritual literature. (Compare, for example, *The Imitation of Christ* with the mystical writings of Ken Wilber, or the guidance of Krishnamurti with the detailed information in the *Rig Veda*.)

The Hindus identify jnana yoga as distinct from bhakti yoga, and Christian spirituality knows the same distinction, respectively, as the wisdom (or gnostic) way and the devotional way. A spiritual master or author of the wisdom/gnostic/jnana path will stress clarified understanding. A master of the devotional/bhakti way will stress affective movements of the heart almost exclusively. Both are equally effective, both valid paths. To achieve the inner "aha" of contemplation, one person will want to understand what's going on and why. To arrive at the same point, another may be led by the heart with no special need for, or interest in, understanding.

The practical corollary for the would-be meditator is, once again: meditate as you can, not as you can't. And if you trod the path of understanding, as explained in this book, be prepared to set your discursiveness aside the moment an invitation to silence beckons.

———

THE SECOND INSIGHT I would share became clear to me after I had studied the history and anthropology of religion for some years. I came to recognize that in the growth and development of human religious thought there are four basic theologies, four generic ways in which people understand and define God. These four understandings have shown up in varieties of cultural dress and myths. And by no means have they always or everywhere appeared in logical sequence. No one knows, for example—and it has been hotly argued—which of the following four understandings of God came first. Did humankind start out in high consciousness and for whatever reason gradually lose it, or are we evolving from spiritual ignorance up to those levels achieved by the most elevated spiritual masters? The important point for all who would learn to meditate, however, is that they appreciate that there is a logical development in the way humans understand the Ultimate Being. This grasp of the process makes it less difficult for them to move into the fourth understanding, where the contemplative experience happens.

First Understanding: By its curious nature, the human mind is driven to search for an adequate explanation and cause of its surrounding and personal reality: "There has to be some sort of adequate cause for everything." The first inclination and attempt at an explanation (logically first, at least, even if not chronologically first) is to identify the Source Being with one or more of the mysterious phenomena surrounding us in the visible universe. Many simple peoples, for example, believe God is a volcano or storm or the ocean or the sun or moon, or that plural gods are both sun and moon. The deity has been variously identified in different cultures and subcultures with whatever seemed to that group to be numinous enough to be a plausible cause of everything.

Second Understanding: On second thought, as it were, it seems more likely to the human mind that any Source Being must be distinctly different from all perceived things and so must be far removed from them, perhaps off in the sky or out in the universe somewhere. In this theology the Ultimate Being is seen as totally beyond the world, completely transcendent.

Third Understanding: With continued growing and still deeper insight, thoughtful and meditative people eventually come to yet another insight about the Source Being. They admit that It is, indeed, transcendent, but they point out that God must also be immanent, that is, must also be present right here beside, with, or even in us. We don't have to cry out across a universe to be heard, because our Creator is, in some mysterious manner, within our hearts and minds. We can, then, as a consequence, speak intimately with our God whenever we wish, and can find unending delight in "practicing the presence of God," as traditional piety in the West puts it. God is, indeed, a separate, transcendent Being, but also, in some marvelous way, present to us as well.

Fourth Understanding: Individual reflective intelligence undoubtedly appeared only rarely in humans during the early stages of the evolution of the race—even though today it is normally present in every toddler. In the same way, a higher or so-called cosmic consciousness has made its appearance in the human race only slowly and even today is relatively rare. As it has appeared in spiritually precocious individuals, however, it has given the race still another level of realization about God. Mystics and enlightened persons move theology to a new level of awareness when, in early times and today, they share their experience and consequent awareness that God is the Being of all things. God is not present *in,* but present *as.* This fourth understanding of God—and the practical corollaries in our lives that flow from it—are what this book is all about.

12

BREAKTHROUGH!

There will come to each of us eventually—sooner if we dare—a vista of insight and pure delight, a vision of our core self, of all others, of the whole cosmos, and of the sweep of human history that is as filled with beauty and peace and joy as it is unprecedented. It's the moment when, after all your reading and thinking and efforts to understand and to still your inner chatter of fear and self-criticism, you realize for the very first time—and in an instant—that all the wonderful theory you've been reading and thinking about is actually true *and applies to you personally.* This first instant of contemplative experience often only lasts for a moment, although literature recounts cases in which it has lasted for hours. It's more usually as if a faint, exotically lovely fragrance wafted for an instant past your nose, or, to use an ancient metaphor, as if a hummingbird fluttered through your vision only long enough to give you a fleeting glimpse of its iridescent colors caught in a ray of sun. Another metaphor out of traditional mystical literature compares first contemplative experiences to a curtain opening onto pure bliss for a fraction of a second, just long enough to allow you the suggestion of a completely new experience.

Spiritual theory is suddenly no longer that. Oneness is henceforward and forever as real for you as anything else in the world. More real. It has suddenly become your personal reality. This is the moment when a meditator moves beyond all the subtle and not-so-subtle fears and legalisms of religious, political, cultural, and familiar storyforms by which he or she has lived and, willy-nilly, been controlled. It's when, for the first time, one sees the whole of the human adventure as a process of unfolding into a growing awareness of its Source— into, that is, what humanity's spiritual tradition calls high consciousness, enlightenment, gnosis, illumination, contemplation, samadhi, satori, bliss, and many other names. You no longer care what people call it, however. All you want to do now is dance.

You see at last that the core you of you is not this conglomerate of incarnational foibles, needs, and uncertainties—not to mention fears and failings—by which you have identified yourself. These are only what has been happening to you. Beneath all such appearances and events there is the ultimate person who is having these experiences. You are not your thoughts or feelings or adventures, but the eternal expression of Existence, the outpost of the divine that is experiencing them. When you were a small child, the real you of you was already there and, unknown to your conscious mind, was having the experiences that you now remember as pleasant or painful. During all your school years, the you of you was there laughing as you made your way through what was put before you to study. Throughout your whole life up to this present moment, the real you of you was there having all your good and "bad" experiences, but never were you the sum of them. At this instant, too, as you read these words, there is a perfectly secure, absolutely confident Self here at the core of your life adventures. It's having these incarnational experiences in the world right now, and within them it forever remains in pure delight over the simple fact of being. The contemplative experience breaks through to your awareness when the realization of this core reality about yourself and all others comes back into your conscious memory.

———

AFTER YOUR FIRST brief contemplative experience, however, you will not yet have completely surrendered to it, and there may well be moments, days, weeks—conceivably years if you only dabble in its pursuit—of repeated returns to uncertainty and searching. Nevertheless, even during these periods of regression into forgetfulness, the fact that you have once glimpsed Reality remains as a brilliant and dancing point of light somewhere deep within your mind and heart. You may not be able to bring it into conscious awareness at will, but neither can you ever, possibly, forget it.

Breakthrough!

———

WHEN IT FINALLY COMES TO US, our new vision of Reality convinces us that the search for ultimate fulfillment has been going on everywhere in all eras. From its beginning, humankind has been muddling through, frantically reaching for peace, security, love, and self-acceptance—legitimate needs, after all. The problem—and your dancing heart doesn't even want any longer to call it a problem, for how can Eternal Being have a problem?—is that it is taking the human race a very long time to learn to fill these realistic needs at a realistic source, that is, at a metaphysically accurate one. Until that happens, humans continue to steal from one another, fight one another, kill one another simply out of ignorance, thinking that only by taking from others can they have enough for themselves. The race has been living in a dangerous nightmare from its beginning, and countless people have been hurt in its flailing. It was in this sense that the Buddha said our only job is to wake up, and that Jesus said it's not to judge, but to love. To wake up is to correct the problem at its source; not to judge is not to misinterpret the problem; to love is to remember the One.

Whether you imagine Stone Age ancestors huddling in the back of a fire-lit cave in the terrors of a forest night, serfs (and lords) eking out meaning in a superstition-riddled medieval countryside, or ermine-clad cardinals engrossed in the pomp of a twentieth-century papal ceremony in Rome—whatever, whenever, wherever, whoever—you see now that our human adventure is at its core independent of particular historical circumstance, and is a grand process of Eternal Being unfolding Itself in the clay of human form and in a history where It returns slowly, inevitably to an awareness of Its Life within matter.

——

As HISTORY HAS UNROLLED, insight after insight has come to our race. Teacher after teacher has added clarifications to our understanding, contributing new storyforms, more equitable political structures, scientific breakthroughs, more workable social contracts. And we have jumped at all of these precisely because of what each promised: an additional step toward fulfillment, toward freedom, peace, security. Some of the philosophies, story-forms, and theories have been singularly accurate, some less so. Some have been off the mark altogether and in the end destructive. Lenin, for example, conceived a good purpose and then sadly misapplied it. Afrikaners honestly believed in their worth and rights, but felt they had to preserve them at another culture's cost. Bits and pieces of eternal wisdom have accumulated in the race, but always with an admixture of mistakes and sometimes the grossest of crimes. New insights often helped us in one way while continuing to subjugate or repress or abuse or steal from us in others.

Our race has made many mistakes, as well as substantial progress. Some new understandings were needed only for a time and eventually outlived their usefulness; others are so basic they are eternal. The sublime spiritual teachings of Zarathustra, Buddha, Jesus, Ramana Maharshi, Eckhart, Krishnamurti come from a deepest grasp of Reality and will last forever. The reflections of individuals like Gandhi and Dag Hammarskjöld have a beyond-time ring to them. The human race is still in the process of walking its long and pain-filled path to remembrance of its Nature, and its wisdom has not come easily or rapidly. But now it's accelerating.

———

Insofar as meditation and the resulting contemplative experience manage to gain a foothold, they bring humankind a fuller vision. The grander perspective they provide shows us that even as stumbling, seemingly half-mad seekers, we are all the while making honest steps on the road to remembering our Origin outside of time. Fulfillment in the most complete sense involves finding all that we ever needed, and the only thing we ever truly wanted.

Human ingenuity has tried all options and gone down countless paths, some sadly mistaken, in its search for fulfillment. We've identified bliss as having more possessions, more pleasure, more power, or as having none of these. We've promised ourselves we'd find bliss if we were humble enough or if we were proud enough; if we owned more things or had a vow of poverty and owned no things; if we had no spouse, exactly one spouse, a sequence of spouses, or many spouses simultaneously. We've despaired at times of ever finding happiness or fulfillment in this lifetime and have decided that wisdom demands cynicism or despair or suicide. Or we've given up any desire for freedom and joy in this world and lived somberly in ritualized religious conformism while waiting for them in the next.

———

BUT THE HUMAN RACE is awakening to the better state of affairs that mystics and enlightened individuals have been telling us about almost from the beginning. We're transcending the limitations of any one culture's storyforms and are outgrowing defensive shortsightedness. We're recognizing the common element in humanity's many wisdom traditions, in each of which we find substantially identical treasures. No matter how or how differently we've gone about it, it was always only bliss all of us were seeking, wisely or not so. We're finally understanding that all wisdoms seek and say essentially the same thing despite whatever defenses still cling to them from our previously pretended, defended, and totally illusory local specialness. With the coming of the contemplative experience, we realize that beneath the variables of history and culture, the bliss we're looking for is not in things or doings, but hidden within ourselves—the last place we thought to look.

Shorn of the circumstances of time, place, and variety of expression, all of the human race is tracking the same scent, driven by the same hunger. Buddhist, Christian, and Hindu monks, along with Jewish Hasidim and Muslim dervishes, are all dancing about the same joy. It is a joy—outrageous, frequently iconoclastic, always compassionate—that feels a need to sing about the vision of human Reality that comes with the experience of God found in meditation.

What Aldous Huxley called humankind's *philosophia perennis,* its "timeless wisdom," runs like a golden thread throughout the tapestry of the human adventure. Nowhere is this more true than in wisdom's highest reach: mysticism. When this most meaningful thread of all is sighted, a person can never again take the variables and superficialities of specific religious, political, or cultural storyforms as anything more than individual variations along the path of humankind's multifaceted search for its deepest and ultimate fulfillment.

13

THE EVOLUTION OF DAWN

It's important and necessary to find, develop, and maintain belief in the promises of universal growth and human enlightenment made in this book, coming as they do out of thousands of years of highest human awareness. It may be a challenge, but it's necessary to believe that the world actually is progressing toward peace and universal goodness despite the cruelty, plagues, risks, genocides, injustices, and self-righteous, destructive bigotries still around us.

Granted, it's difficult to have faith in the promise of a beautiful sunrise during a night of tornadoes, but on pain of incapacitating ourselves and despairing of our race in fear and hopelessness, we must do exactly that. Storms always do pass, the sun always does come up—and sunrises are always things of great glory. It's difficult to believe that families broken by violence can ever be healed, but if we don't see that potential, we will give up during domestic crises, many of which are eventually solved. Those working with disturbed families see remarkable recoveries time after time. Moreover, anyone working with families knows that most healing happens because a family member or therapist kept on believing, kept on trying. It was difficult for me to believe that some of the severely wounded and profoundly disturbed Vietnam returnees with whom I worked for several years could ever again feel good about life, could ever actively, successfully take part in it again. And yet I saw that transformation take place in the vast majority of them. I also watched as one particularly skillful counselor grew increasingly despondent and angry at what had been done to these men and women, and eventually withdrew from working with them. He capitulated to a too-narrow view of the possibilities in their futures. His failure serves as a warning to all of us concerning the dangers of narrow horizons and shortened perspectives.

The Evolution of Dawn

Listeners sometimes accuse me of unrealistic optimism after public talks in which I have spoken enthusiastically of the growing enlightenment and bright future of humanity. This is a difficult objection to answer in a convincing manner to those both unfamiliar with the history and data of human contemplative spirituality and lacking the personal spiritual experience that reaffirms what that history shows. To reply to them, I suggest that we must never limit our view of possibilities by our present store of knowledge. Simple comparisons underline that principle. A century ago, no one would have thought it possible to have breakfast in New York, lunch in Chicago, and dinner in San Francisco all on the same day. People had no way then of suspecting the coming jet planes, just as we today can scarcely conceive of the teleportation devices some scientists predict for tomorrow. The common error is to presume that tomorrow's means of travel cannot surpass today's. Another example: Science fiction writers in the 1920s proclaimed that one day we'd land on the moon, but my junior-high-school science text pictured an airplane flying off toward the moon with this authoritative caption: "Man will never reach the moon because his fastest flying machine would take seventy-two years to get there."

As human genius produces new technologies, it applies them immediately and only later learns how to harness them into harmlessness. Nuclear power, for example, is an unlimited resource at a time when we need it, but the first thing we did after discovering it was to use it to incinerate hundreds of thousands of people. It's myopic, nevertheless, to recognize only that crime and our slow development of safety measures for the use of it and to forget its potential benefits. How many people died in early aircraft as we were learning the intricacies of aerodynamics? How many people still die as new, near-miraculous medicines are used before all of their long-term side effects are recognized? Can you imagine modern life without the availability of fire, but how many caves were gutted and huts burned before early humans learned how to use it safely?

———

The Evolution of Dawn

TODAY'S WORLD IS, indeed, challenged by many colossal problems. In view of how we've handled both ourselves and our planet to date, there is ample reason for despair . . . if human technology were all we had to work with and the example of human conduct thus far all we could realistically hope for. Fortunately, human technology is *not* our only resource, and you can't judge the potential of a race by its adolescent years. As time passes and the race matures, we're learning to recognize a spiritual vision and to call upon our spiritual resources. Optimism and confidence in today's world are unintelligible unless we accept the reality of our shared Eternal Existence and thereby embrace our innate superabundant resources and our assurance of ultimate fulfillment.

Some reject this contemplative view of humanity and its challenges because they imagine that if we see human atrocities and failings as mistakes on a path to something greater, we will no longer put tough laws and appropriate sanctions in place for these mistaken actions. Contemplative spirituality requires no such silliness. As long as the illusion lingers of humans being less than what we are, we will continue to have to deal with the results of that illusion. Jails and other appropriate sanctions will be required until people have graduated from all fear and the self-confusion that pushes them to seek security and abundance at the expense of others. The world and its problems—and problem individuals—are not "evil" and "bad"; they are confused and in error—horrific error at times. And, yet, the golden rule of all world spiritualities, that we love our enemies, will always be true, for we are all one. That is why the Buddha required universal compassion of us. He said nothing, however, about letting harmful people roam freely. He only said to compassionate them until they wake up.

———

DESPITE TODAY'S FAULTS, failures, and flubs, the direction the race is taking is undeniably upward, forward. Global communication is fighting back tribe-based isolation and blood-drenched defensiveness. For the first time, the world is recognizing itself as a place of legitimate pluralities. Intercultural commerce, sharing of information, exchange of students are common today and are creating a global mutuality of knowledge and respect. A medical breakthrough in Paris or Atlanta today is used in the South Seas and Lesotho tomorrow. Each of the world's nations reads other national literatures and openly appreciates unfamiliar cultural forms. When I was a child adults routinely despised and laughed at the unfamiliar of other cultures. It was considered a matter to be ridiculed that men wore "skirts" in Scotland and women wore "trousers" in China. A violent repression of students in a foreign city that would have gone unnoticed and largely without compassion yesterday causes international outrage today. Tomorrow it will be unthinkable. We no longer take it for granted, as medieval society did, that there are trolls under bridges, devils in the mentally disturbed, divine punishment upon lepers. We no longer believe it to be God's will that we put conquered populations to death, even though—as the Bible makes abundantly clear—that is exactly what was understood to be a divine imperative four thousand years ago. We still do horrific things today, like dropping napalm and defoliating agents, and we have atomic, biological, and chemical weapons of war. No one today would claim that the use of such instruments is a good thing. Some may still consider them a necessary recourse under certain circumstances, but the ethical level of world thinking now agrees that they must be used only as a last recourse, if at all. This development of thought represents remarkable progress in our moral understanding, which, as history shows, has always been way out in front of our practice.

There was a day when serfs sat quietly by and accepted the burden that layers of powerful rulers loaded upon them and that their church explained was their duty to submit to in this world. In the same breath, the same church was telling kings it was their divine right to rule. The Christian Testament itself tells slaves to be willingly subject to their masters. Despite this long habituation to backwardness, however, human awareness and ethical sensitivity have moved past justifying such injustices. In many places, it is true, human practice still falters, but human awareness has pushed ahead and continues to do so.

14

GETTING STARTED

After thirteen chapters of what I consider to be essential and foundational material in a rather short book about meditation, we have finally arrived at the "how to" part of the discussion. Even at this point, I reluctantly present any guidance about specifics. I don't want readers to "follow rules" in their search *instead of understanding the process and how it works* and then do as they wish to activate that process in their lives. I'll write as much as I must, therefore, and no more than I should. This will be little enough, I fondly hope, that it won't turn you away from enjoying freedom and spontaneity when you meditate.

My convictions about teaching meditation now that I'm an older man are directly opposite those I

believed as a young man. Then, I wanted somebody—anybody!—to spell out for me exactly and in
the greatest possible detail what in hell I was supposed to do during meditation. Today I would
counsel that young firebrand to keep working on his
insights and understandings, to spend time every day
in composure and thoughtfulness, to be alert to
abandon his mind for his heart when interiorly invited to do so, and not to worry about the rest.
George the Younger would never have been satisfied
with such vague guidance from George the Older.
I understand completely if readers who dished out
good money for this book are initially dismayed at
the slim fare this chapter contains in the way of
specific guidance on how to meditate. But, as I have
explained, that trimmed-down approach (which I
have found to be singularly successful) was my de-
clared justification for writing yet another book on
meditation. My experience and the good things that
have come to me via meditation assure me that this
brevity is a significant favor to readers. I will provide their effort to meditate vastly more benefit with
the following succinct paragraph than were I to pro-
duce a huge tome of specific dos and don'ts.

Getting Started

Your highest bliss and eternal fulfillment already exist within you, as you. Your sole and simple task—so simple as to be elusive—is to recognize this inner Reality and no longer imagine that you are a spiritual pauper required to embark on a lengthy search to find your wholeness and happiness elsewhere.

———

HERE ARE some ways you may wish to begin. Don't let these suggestions become rules. Be as creative as you like. Modify what follows to suit yourself in any manner you find helpful. There are no rules, only sublime possibilities.

1. Determine, first, that you will not make your effort more complicated than necessary. Meditation, like other new things, may seem highly involved initially, but bear in mind that the process itself is never complex. It may take you time to become proficient even in the most generalized practice that is suggested below (and you are invited to do *anything* that works for you), but always move away from difficult techniques and in the direction of simple experiencing. And remember, if you learn to control your thoughts perfectly, to fill yourself with sublime and ab-

sorbing images, if you sit and breathe with flawless rhythm, if you manage to be quiet and astonishing in your bodily and mental discipline, you are still not a contemplative. Indeed, if you obsess on such trivialities, you may very well never become one. Don't be duped into giving techniques or appearances an importance they don't have—either when you master all of the above or when you fail to master any of it.

2. Schedule as much time as you peacefully and realistically can to realize results in an expeditious manner without swamping your boat. Because you are seeking a new way of seeing the reality of your life, five minutes every day will be significantly more effective than two hours once a week. You need *frequent* reminders if you are going to revise your old habits of thought. And while five minutes is acceptable, ten is better. Schedule a time brief enough that if your effort is confusing and tedious at first, it won't cause you to abandon your resolve and give up the process altogether. As you sense the first fruits of your effort, the five, ten, or fifteen minutes you initially dedicate to meditation each day (both morning and evening if you can swing it) will spontaneously lengthen without signifi-

cant effort on your part. You will find yourself hooked on so rewarding a practice.

3. Find your favorite chair, or if it's comfortable to do so, sit cross-legged on a pillow that is just thick enough to raise your butt two or three inches off the floor (this helps keep your spine straight). Many people find they can sit comfortably for a protracted time in this position. Others say they can't sit that way at all. Postures, like other techniques, are variable. It makes no difference if you kneel, sit in lotus, or hang from a chandelier when meditating, as long as the body is comfortable enough to permit your mind and heart the freedom they need. (That rules out hanging from chandeliers for most of us.) Unless you are something of a human hinge, I suggest you don't start off trying to sit in the perfect-lotus position. There's no divine reward for experiencing the great pain of having your legs tied in a square knot. The position you ultimately settle on must remain your choice, however, so be sure of your decision. Also, situate yourself where you won't be interrupted by people, phones, or pets—especially cats, who seem to enjoy taking advantage of people who are meditating.

4. If music in the background helps, have it. If it doesn't, don't. There's no right or wrong, better or worse about the use of music for meditation. The day will come when you won't want it, but by then you will be too absorbed in something else to be bothered by it even if you do notice it.

5. Should you spend this allotted time for meditation in pondering the ideas discussed in earlier chapters? If you understand that question to ask if you should be trying to remember the conclusions of someone else's thinking, then the answer is no. Meditation is not a classroom exercise. If, however, you understand the question to ask if you should work at deeper metaphysical understanding until you are gently invited by the motion of your spirit to something more simple, then the answer is yes. Emphatically yes. You are wise to use your meditation time initially to try to *understand* the nature of the universe. In the early practice of meditation you will be better off spending your time thinking and reasoning than just waiting for something to happen as, perhaps, you count your breaths, repeat a mantra, "contemplate" your navel, or stare into the depths of a flower or flame. Detailed thinking, with or without the help of a book, will always be only

a beginner's ploy, but it's one that should be maintained as long as it's helpful. Use water wings as long as you need them to learn to swim, but get rid of them as soon as you can, or you will never know the joy of riding a surf.

6. Relax your body. This only takes a moment or less, but it's important. A short and effective way to relax—and to check periodically during your quiet time to see if you are still relaxed—is to settle *consciously* into gravity. Try to feel gravity more than you ever have. This doesn't suggest that you should slouch, but only that in being attentive, you do so effortlessly. Tenseness never serves any good purpose, least of all when you want to meditate. Relaxing into gravity is a useful way to release all bodily tensions. Another simple way to relax is to check the muscles in your face. If they are relaxed, your body is relaxed. Just the suggestion of a smile—not a grin, but a smile—is an effective way to ensure that your face is relaxed.

7. Insofar as possible, whenever you begin your meditation, try without pressure to be thoroughly and consciously present to yourself in the present moment, no matter what your state of mind and heart. Strive not to leave the now by

leaning back out of it into the past in guilt or by leaning forward out of it into the future in anxiety. Stay in the present. *Remind yourself that the point of being in meditation is not to see how much of the Presence of God you can bring into your life—for It is already wholly there—but how much of your life you can bring into the present where It is.* Don't worry if your mind and imagination are racing about, but do turn away from any *deliberate* mental nonsense. You will find your inner noise eventually disappearing, but for now, peacefully and repeatedly, turn away from it by turning to something else with the help of a book, if necessary, as described below. Any time you spend trying to reply to, or reason with, fear, hurt, anger, worry, and so on, is completely wasted, totally ineffective, and, indeed, counterproductive to any effort to meditate.

8. Without pressuring yourself or worrying about failure, open a previously selected spiritual book and see if it will serve to lead you into a realization of your identification with your Source (for suggested readings, see Appendix A). Slowly read through a brief section and pause with it as long as it holds your attention or engages your feelings. Remain with it as long as possible, but move freely on as soon as necessary. The point here is

not to think, but to experience, so don't read merely from curiosity, but from a desire to experience something of the Ultimate Reality that, perhaps, you've never experienced before. Make sure that the books you choose for this purpose are not mere rehashings of the biblical view of God as a separate, patriarchlike master artisan and legislator. By the very fact that you are trying to meditate, you will want the images and insights in the books you select to help you get past the literal content of those earlier storyforms. If what you read engages your attention and/or feelings, stay with that experience as long as you can. When, *and only if,* the experience dries up, go on to a next option.

9. Remind yourself that you don't have to succeed at meditation (or anything else!) to be secure in the universe. Don't feel as if you're a failure if you don't have what you still understand to be a "good" meditation. You are honestly trying to learn to walk in things spiritual. Rather than criticize yourself for the ups and downs of your time of learning, respect yourself deeply for being on the path at all. Tell yourself that whether you can meditate today or not, you share God's Life nonetheless. The fact of the most

basic Fact of your life is still a fact, whether you are at the moment feeling it or not. Gently, firmly clarify your goals: "I am trying to develop my conscious awareness of spiritual reality. I intend to learn to meditate and to come to that condition of human fulfillment called enlightenment. I have never before been so close to a clear grasp of fulfillment and happiness. I intend to work on this endeavor as a whole person. For these moments, then, I plan to attend to spiritual realities, rather than to the material and physical matters that have preoccupied me for so long."

10. If you are unable to turn away successfully from distractions, don't berate yourself for it. Something you must learn as quickly as possible is that you must not beat up on yourself for this or for anything whatsoever. Even if you experience nothing, meditative reading and the mere intentional withdrawal from your customary routine are seeding your mind for another day when you will, indeed, experience much. Be most alert to ensure that you don't willingly allow yourself to feel at fault if you don't "succeed."

11. Don't let stress in your life torment you; meditation is possible amid troubles. Recalling the fact that you are an outpressing of Eternal Being,

present here as you, is just as possible in a state of turmoil as it is in one of peace—not as easy (at first), but just as possible. *Your Eternal Reality can never be undone or curtailed by any thought or feeling.* If you consciously work for a short time to develop the habit of remembering this fact, it becomes no more difficult to keep it habitually in mind than it is, for example, to recall—with equal ease during times of peace and joy and in times of great turmoil—that you are male or female, as your case may be. In both instances, you are simply recalling a fact.

12. Gently try to enter into a sense of closeness to God. Simply recall the fact of who and what you are—one with the Ultimate One of all reality. See yourself as the consciousness beneath all your activity, your problems, your successes, your personal history. You are the thinker beneath your thoughts. Beneath distractions and troubles, let the fact of your underlying core Nature slowly begin to register with you. If the sense of closeness to Eternal Reality happens, be grateful and stay with this experience as long as you can. When, *and only if,* it dries up or never gets started, move on without panic or recrimination to what follows.

13. If, as your time set aside for meditation draws to a close, you seem to have achieved nothing, face an important fact. You are *learning* to meditate, and substantial, patient effort is involved in learning anything of great value. Determine to keep trying. Decide firmly not to be discouraged. The advice in this chapter is designed to help you get started meditating, not to establish norms by which you will lower your self-esteem should you fail to achieve them promptly. The most important advice of all about meditation is this: Don't give up. Keep trying. Be inventive. Be creative. Remind yourself that even great masters began at the beginning. (How many more great masters would there be had nobody who ever started on the path of meditation given up?) Resolve anew to keep at your search for total enlightenment.

———

YOU MAY FIND IT HELPFUL during your meditation to remind yourself occasionally that there is only One Reality, One Being, One Life, and that that Reality, that Being, that Life is also yours. It's What's outpressing here as you.

Remember over and over: You don't have to acquire, only to realize. The sole point of meditation is to realize Who and What you *already* Are.

And, consequently, that all is well.

Forever, already well.

15

―――――

KEEPING THE VISION

I used to hear elderly Catholic parishioners in San Francisco use a traditional Irish greeting, "Keep the faith." In a previous era—and perhaps still today in some places—it was a reminder and warm wish from one believer to another that they be true to their common understanding of God's requirements as they were spelled out to them by their church. In light of what this book has been discussing, however, "Keep the *vision*" is a more appropriate expression of this loving concern. And it's certainly no mere whimsical wish. Keeping in mind the overview, the vision of the greater and cosmic reality in which we exist is an effective— and perhaps the only—way to establish complete stability and optimism in our daily lives, to find and hang onto lightheartedness and a sense of well-being.

When pain, confusion, and anxiety seem to become overwhelming, many people find themselves running after the snake oil of mind- or body-altering drugs, clinging to shamelessly self-enraptured preachers, or rushing to overpriced quick-fix seminars. They jump at any and every promise of relief, of "salvation" in any immediate sense. Some are so confused about the alleged rules of the game on earth that they are even willing to listen seriously when a teacher or organization tells them that real relief will (or may) come only after death. That irrational opinion is the ultimate cynicism exercised upon the universe, the grossest affront to its Source Being, and the most destructive of all human abuses because it destroys from the root any belief in the possibility of completely healing human ills in this world. If this world were a place of fear and relative unimportance as some religions teach, there would, indeed, be room for cynicism and despair. But it is not.

If the cure for Western society's malformation in fear and self-criticism lies in finding a revised understanding, a new grasp of—a new vision of—the reality in which we live and of which we are a part, finding that vision is the work of meditation. It gives us a more informed, more complete outlook on ourselves and on everything else. It corrects first impressions, undoes faulty formation, puts a spotlight on cynical interpretations, and provides us our own, not somebody else's, *experience* of the nature of reality.

———

AND WHEN WE FINALLY do begin to see our life context and circumstances independent of learned negativity, it becomes our responsibility to keep this vision.

Maintaining a spiritual view of reality does not involve walking about in a zombielike state of abstraction, feet no longer on the ground, silly grins on our faces, detached from the doings of this earth. It doesn't imply that we no longer take this world, its citizens, its environment, its daily duties seriously. It implies exactly the opposite. It causes each of us to realize that Existence is happening,

Life is living, Bliss is burgeoning right here in this present moment and in this immediate involvement and activity.

Nor does keeping the vision mean that we must walk around with a clarified metaphysical understanding in the focus of our attention at each moment. If that were so, we would be able to give only partial attention to daily living. A true vision of reality is never out of sync with that reality. It is always and in every way a vision of and response to what actually is. Keeping the vision doesn't predetermine what we think about each moment, but it does determine what we *realize* each moment, whether we are thinking about it or not. Something that we realize can be out of the central focus of our thought and yet totally dominate our lives. If you have, for example, the "realization" that you are flawed and inferior, you don't have to be thinking about this psychological guilt every minute for it to ruin your whole day, your whole life. In the same way, if you have the realization that your Reality is spelled with a capital *R* and that you share Its security and abundance and eternal well-being, you don't need to be thinking about it every minute for it to inform and transform your life. As we begin to keep the new vision, we begin to accept ourselves completely. We no longer build our self-estimate on whether or not we are physically advantaged, wealthy, or approved by others, for now we are forming our self-estimate on the nature of our *inner* being.

———

ONE OF THE FIRST RESULTS of a corrected and spiritual view of Reality will be that we find ourselves beginning to walk, talk, and live each moment with the poise of genuine self-respect and security. This poise is not something we can call up at will or learn by self-control. If we go after it in that way, we will be imposing it on ourselves by restraining spontaneity and creativity. Our new poise will be a pose. It will be strained because it will be pasted on and not something naturally flowing from inner conviction and insight. True poise is an inside job. It comes from recognized personal possession of wholeness and essential security. It's always spontaneous, unaffected, lighthearted, genuine, loving. As personal recognition deepens and develops, inner and outer poise grows apace.

You will still forget the new vision at times, of course, and give way to old habits and old fears, but these moments are only passing mistakes and no longer a way of life. If you are addicted—to alcohol, nicotine, other drugs, or to codependency, for example—you will find yourself springing free. A person with genuine spiritual insight doesn't have to go through long and uncertain efforts to conquer addictions, because the final and only total cure of destructive addictions is not giving up something, but finding something: oneself. The healing we seek from spirituality is being promised not as though coming from outside, but from within ourselves, from our own experience and realization. Insofar as we find enlightenment, we find the only thing we were looking for all along, and we find it close at hand. We readily toss out unneeded substitutes.

Even after meditation has begun to perk for you, you will probably (there are exceptions) not wake up one morning and be suddenly and totally changed. Meditation is usually an unfolding process, the process of recognizing a new vision, of realizing how all things fit in it, and of gradually experiencing the resulting ramifications. Don't berate yourself when you fail. Be patient during your process . . . although not so patient that you render it ineffective. The results it will bring about in your life are inevitable as long as you keep meditating and *gently* trying to see things more clearly. During one of his daily talks in the monastery where I lived as a monk for many years, our old abbot warned us novices to be patient, not to try to build Rome in a single day. Then, looking over the top of his reading glasses and out over the senior monks, he added, "On the other hand, some of you older monks might speed up a little." A balance is needed.

———

KEEP, BUT ALSO USE, THE VISION. Gently, consistently strive to realize that the *core* you of you, and of everybody else, is forever secure, abundant, free of distress because everyone shares the only Existence there is. Don't let this Oneness remain just a theory in your life. You possess worth and beauty quite independently of anything you have ever done or left undone. You have it because of what you *Are* and not at all because of any talents or objects you possess or deeds you have accomplished. And absolutely nothing whatsoever, no one whosoever, can take it from you.

Your life is your living of Life. That is the same as saying that the purpose of your being is your process. God is a verb, and so, therefore, are you. You are an unfolding. You are Eternal Life coming to full awareness of Itself from within matter. You are not at risk. The reason to keep this vision and to work on it is so you will not delay your fulfillment and its joy. *Your goal is not to arrive somewhere, but to be aware of where you already are.* Your process already contains your Goal. If you still imagine that meditation is going to give you something you don't already have, you're missing the point of this book. The kingdom of God is *already* within you, so don't waste your lifetime searching for it elsewhere. The vision you are to keep requires that you act now as though you already have what you're after—*because you do.* Only your fuller realization of all this remains to be found.

The *experience* of spiritual fulfillment, of bliss, comes not when we acquire it, but when we re-member it.

———

KEEPING THE VISION is not asking us to remember what may happen to us, but what already has.

16

SUNRISE

As humanity's storyform about a powerful, demanding, and sometimes dangerously upset God is
slowly replaced for both individuals and world society, what will fill its place? As the human race
continues its movement into political, economic,
and informational unity—first in theory and only
then in practice—what will its image of its Ultimate Origin look like? How will the new understanding of our Source Being express itself? This
shift will be difficult, not because of what has to be
learned, but because of what has to be unlearned.
Deprogramming kids hooked into a severely abusive cult is child's play when compared to the task
of deprogramming a whole culture that for centuries has believed the story about an offended

God, a glory-hungry King in the sky, a Judge with a supply of worms that don't die and an eternal jail set in the midst of flames, a God who—oh, by the way—was also said to be loving.

The answer is simple: The future spiritual understanding of humanity will unfold along the lines spiritual giants have traced for millennia.

An insightful way to appreciate humanity's more spiritual understanding of God is to ask how it will function in light of that understanding.

Awakened humanity will deal with its God as the intimate Source of its Life and Being in each moment, and no longer deal with "Him" as a separate ruler. Its grown-up view of Ultimate Reality will involve a return to the present from its old way of leaning into the past in guilt and into the future in anxiety. It will firmly place its attention into a relaxed (and lighthearted) present. Increasing numbers of individuals—and so, gradually, society as a whole—will realize that life is found totally, *and only,* in each succeeding instant. We will know that fullest living is not a goal to be reached, but an awareness to be remembered. Here, in this present moment and in these unique circumstances—as you are reading this page, for example—we will see ourselves as a simple branching of the stream of Eternal Existence.

Previous images and concepts of gods or God as understood in the childhood of the race served to move it a bit along the way to today, but in the future we will put away the things of children. A million faces for God were used in India, a single face among the Hebrews and Muslims, a Trinity of faces for Christians, no face at all for Buddhists and Taoists, and faces of uncounted varieties elsewhere. The day is upon us when, as when snow transforms what hours ago was the dying countryside of late autumn, the human landscape will be graced with a new and unified beauty in both understanding and ethical, social, political practice.

———

HUMANITY IS STILL FAR—in distance, although not necessarily in time—from achieving this universal enlightenment, but it is vastly closer than it was a millennium ago, a century ago, a decade ago. We began the trek toward enlightenment the day a probably wordless caveman first sensed a fleeting feeling of remorse at having killed his neighbor to have his wife. It was still moving forward hundreds of thousands of years later when his sister of today wondered if she should, perhaps, have been more patient in dealing with her neighbor. It moves ahead each time a moment of reflection leads anyone anywhere to ask if there isn't a better, more just, more compassionate, more insightful way to do something. "Isn't there a more loving way to react?" The process of human spiritual development lunges forward, especially, each time a spiritual master in any era comes to enlightenment in any significant degree and then goes on to help humankind be a bit more conscious of the unseen world, a bit more thoughtful about meaningful ways to relate to Ultimate Reality, a bit more concerned about effective ways to reduce human strain, competition, and fear.

——

BEFORE MEDITATION LIFTS US into the contemplative experience, to the cosmic consciousness and

joy that is called enlightenment, it always first ac-
complishes a more immediate task. It gives us a
perspective on ourselves and on others as being not
failures and sinners, but struggling individuals who
make mistakes. It teaches us compassion and pa-
tience and eventually perfect love, not only for
others, but also for ourselves. It reveals the human
race not as evil or on a path to self-destruction, but
as a distressed child struggling with fear and insecurity as it slowly focuses on the bigger picture and
finds, at last, its sense of innate dignity and ultimate
safety.

At the future point when this transformation
will have been accomplished in us—not because
of an arbitrary decree by an alleged supreme ruler,
but simply by the activation of the potential in our
hearts and minds—we will *feel* as never before the
urge to provide for everyone in whatever way
falls within our ability. Providing for others will
no longer be the patronizing act of a charity divinely mandated, but a simple corollary of our
having recognized Who and What all of us are.
From the resulting mutual esteem and recognized
parity, the human race will move forward to-

gether to fill all its needs for food, warmth, shelter, loving support, intimate companionship, and—because of the largess of Eternal Being that is not about to run out of things—all its meaningful wants as well.

———

INSTEAD OF LEAVING us to damn our situation and tremble in the long frozen winter of human greed and the fear built on the illusion of our innate poverty and evil, meditation leads us, soon enough, to hear the new life pushing up everywhere through the frozen soil. Joy and deeper respect are rising into human focus and feelings across the width of the world. Be watchful and notice, not because it is demanded of you, but lest you miss any more of a party that has long since begun. Be aware. Recognize everywhere that the winter is almost over and past and flowers are appearing in our land. Be glad for your neighbors, for alien peoples, for the atmosphere, the woodlands, the forests, the animals. For yourself. And especially for trusting little children whose simpler wisdom and straighter sight have too often been betrayed and their toys beat into things of war.

It is clear to a thoughtful observer that the world and its human race are in the process of healing. The lessons of the Berlin Wall, South Africa's apartheid, and Russia's Bolshevik Revolution have deeper implications than momentary reprieve. The sunrise is well advanced and the warmth of a new day on earth is dawning upon us. If there are many places still locked in the shadows, the sun is rising nonetheless. Centuries of illusions are evaporating like hoarfrost on leafless bushes surprised in a brilliant dawn.

EPILOGUE

────

Close the eyes of your body and look out on the earth with those of your spirit. Consider carefully what you see.

Be glad and grateful that you are among those invited to witness the passing of fear. Don't tremble and prolong its life as you hear the great howl it releases as its kingdom melts in the warmth of a glorious aurora of human consciousness. Smile and be happy deep within. Join the rain forests and atmosphere and whales as they rejoice that humankind is at last awakening to what harm it was loading upon them. In your spirit hear them singing again as they did before our arrival . . . and not for their own returning welfare only, but also for that of their human siblings.

LEARNING TO DANCE INSIDE

All is calm and well beneath our storm.
Notice this.
Join the dance.

And learn to meditate so you can.

Appendix A

————

SPIRITUAL READING

The importance of meditative reading can be summed up in a series of related statements:

What we live by depends on what we believe.
What we believe depends on what we understand.
What we understand depends on what we know.
What we know depends on what we are exposed to.
What we are exposed to largely depends on what we read.

————

It's essential to undertake a program of spiritual reading if we plan to pursue spiritual growth and search for the contemplative experience with any realistic expectation of success. Only by broadening and deepening our database, only by deliberately exposing our minds to spiritual considerations will we expand our understanding and appreciation to include the full sweep of reality, spiritual as well as material. In that way we will overcome the generalized illusion of the human race that the world is a dangerous place, that others are our competitors and judges, and that we are essentially weak, impoverished, and in jeopardy.

———

UNTIL THE SECOND QUARTER of the twentieth century, two books dominated religious reading in the Western world, the Bible and *The Imitation of Christ,* an early-fifteenth-century book, second only to the Bible in popularity for many centuries. Spiritual appetites have significantly expanded and changed since then, and today the printing industry is busy responding to a vastly expanded and more sophisticated market. When I began as a campus minister in 1985 at the University of Washington in Seattle, the three-story university bookstore had only a few shelf yards of books related to spirituality. Today it has whole sections of such books, and a nearby wholesale supplier has a warehouse twice as big as most gymnasiums filled with nothing but books related to spirituality. Books of this kind are currently so plentiful that you will have no difficulty in locating reading to your liking.

No matter how remarkable its content, variety, and availability, however, even the most sublime spiritual writing will do you no good unless you read it. Undertaking a spiritual-reading program may be intimidating at first, but once you start, you will find yourself hooked and enthusiastically launched on a path of feeding your internal computer with ever-expanding spiritual insight. If the first book you choose doesn't adequately engage your mind and heart, try another. Not one of us bats a thousand all the time. Reading is one of most important resources at your disposal for spiritual development.

———

DON'T READ COMPULSIVELY just because I and others insist so confidently that you should read. *Read only because you want to understand.*

And read critically. With a little moxie and not much money, anybody can get a book into print today. The words of Francis Bacon in his essay "Of Studies" were never more applicable: "Some books are to be tasted, others to be swallowed, and some few to be chewed and digested."

Start with the topic that most attracts you. You're not reading to pass a test, but to get yourself involved and your interest aroused. Understanding and conviction—and then contemplation—will follow.

Be aware that if you choose church-published books, they will, with few exceptions, contain political, organization, and doctrinal hype that will serve you not at all in updating your vision of Reality and achieving the contemplative experience. Read courageously and choose your own fare no matter what vested interests are eager to select your reading for you.

———

HERE ARE SOME SPIRITUAL BOOKS that many find particularly insightful.

Appendix A

As a sampling of the mystic efforts and successes of the human race, Lex Hixon's *Coming Home: The Experience of Enlightenment in Sacred Traditions* is among the best. Another is John White's *What is Enlightenment: Exploring the Goal of the Spiritual Path*. For an in-depth study of the nature and role of mysticism in human history, W.T. Stace's *Mysticism and Philosophy* is classic. Aldous Huxley's *The Perennial Philosophy* is arguably the best-ever anthology of world mystical traditions.

On the same subject, but at a more abstract level—explaining what underlies all mysticism—Alan Watts's *This Is It* (actually only one essay in a book that carries the essay's name) provides an excellent discussion of contemplative spirituality.

For anyone wanting a detailed overview of Christianity as practiced for centuries, and as distinct from the original spirituality of earlier times, *Original Blessing: A Primer in Creation Spirituality* by Matthew Fox is singularly insightful.

Two books will be helpful to those who want an introduction to the so-called new physics in so far as it affects spirituality—as it certainly does. Gary Zukav's *The Dancing Wu Li Masters: An*

Overview of the New Physics, and Danah Zohar's *The Quantum Self: Human Nature and Consciousness Defined by the New Physics.* Both take concentrated reading, but they are worth the effort.

Some authors, like Wayne Dyer, have a knack for introducing spirituality with a coating of self-help psychology. His book *Real Magic* deals with various levels of self-healing, but it's filled with practical expressions of and applications of the best of the world's spiritual wisdom. Several books by Deepak Chopra, like his *Quantum Healing* and his *Unconditional Life,* and the books of Jerry Jampolsky, like his *Love is Letting Go of Fear,* do the same thing. Richard Moss has written a superb summary of transformative personal spirituality, *The I That is We: Awakening to Higher Energies Through Unconditional Love.*

Ken Wilber has written many outstanding books that help raise one's consciousness, but none is more complete than his *The Atman Project: A Transpersonal View of Human Development.* This is not an easy book, and it probably should not be the first book of someone just embarking on a program of spiritual reading.

Appendix A

Be circumspect if you decide to read books from the New Age shelves in bookstores, but don't reject all of them out of hand. Just be aware that enthusiastic hype over strangeness is not a dependable path to the contemplative experience. Some of these books, however, even when "channeled," are excellent, like those of Ken Carey, Emmanuel, and Bartholomew.

———

COUNTLESS OTHER BOOKS could be listed here; the reading list I provide during workshops runs to many pages. My experience with students of meditation, however, is that only general suggestions for a first book are needed. Once one senses the delight that flows from convincing insights and the relief that accompanies critical religious thought and personal spirituality, there is slight chance that a meditator's reading program will flounder.

———

LEARNING TO DANCE INSIDE

THERE DOES COME A TIME when it is appropriate and necessary to move beyond spiritual reading. *Nothing* along the spiritual path should be made into an idol and clung to forever. There's an amusing, but meaningful, incident in the most recent film version of W. Somerset Maugham's *The Razor's Edge,* in which Bill Murray plays Larry, the leading role. During his monastic episode in the Orient, Larry is sent by his elderly Buddhist abbot to a mountain ashram for a time of solitary meditation. When he arrives at the snow-bound, windswept stone hermitage, he finds nothing with which to build a fire to keep warm. Slowly an awful realization dawns on him, and we watch a smile form on his face as he realizes why the abbot had him take along his books: the only material available to burn. He lights a fire and page by page frees himself from his heretofore inseparable companions. The abbot knew that the day had come when his young American aspirant was ready to find within himself what he had until then thought he could find only in books.

Knowing when to fold is as important in the practice of spiritual reading as it is in poker. Stop reading when it becomes a drudgery, when it is no longer something that is clearly helping you along the path. On that day you will have learned to listen to your deepest Self faithfully and habitually, and you will know clearly that reading has become superfluous. It is, for sure, necessary to read broadly, but there comes a time when it's equally necessary to put aside your dependence on books. When you have learned the basic facts and important details that spiritual books have to teach you, get out from under them, out of your intellect, and into the personal experience of what you've been reading about.

Appendix B

KEEPING A SPIRITUAL JOURNAL

Spiritual journaling is an important and effective bridge between two points in time: when you need books and when you need to be free of them.

———

A CHINESE PROVERB READS:

> *Hearing, I forget.*
> *Seeing, I remember.*
> *Writing, I understand.*

Keeping a private journal of one's spiritual insights and lessons is called journaling. It's a powerful way to foster understanding since it helps us make our own what we read and learn during meditation. Here are some guidelines to help you gain the most benefits when you journal.

LEARNING TO DANCE INSIDE

———

IN A SPIRITUAL JOURNAL—as distinct from diaries and other types of personal records that concern themselves with problems, relationships, and the like—aspirants to high consciousness record and work to assimilate the spiritual understandings that are coming to them. Spiritual journaling supplements spiritual reading. Journaling helps us understand what books and meditation are showing us.

There are many advantages in recording spiritual insights and copying out particularly helpful passages from favorite spiritual books. What is crystal clear today may be forgotten and irretrievable tomorrow. Some days we seem to be flapping about as if riding the tail of a kite. It's helpful at such times to have a familiar book of our best insights (our journal) from which we can review realizations we had on days when we seemed to be coasting like an eagle riding effortlessly on air currents.

———

Appendix B

THERE IS ONE CARDINAL RULE about keeping a spiritual journal: *Never write anything negative in it.* If journaling turns into a diary of self-criticism, no matter how otherwise helpful it may be, it will cease to be *spiritually* helpful. Psychological note keeping in which our problems and other negative matters are recorded and discussed is sometimes helpful, although there is always a risk associated with focusing on the negative. But even if and when this kind of diary seems useful, it is not a spiritual journal, and the two should not be confused. A spiritual journal is wholly and solely oriented to spiritual insight and understanding, to what is, by its nature, positive and healing about our deepest selves. Spiritual journals should deal solely with information about our innermost Nature. As some spiritual giant I read once said, it's not by looking at our sores that we are healed, but by contemplating Beauty. Keep your sights on the goal. Don't look backward at yesterday's (or this morning's) mistakes, or forward at the awful things you imagine may happen tomorrow. Stick to the point!

———

DON'T SHARE YOUR JOURNAL with anyone other than a trusted spiritual guide, if you have one. It's essential that your writing be motivated solely by a search for personal insight and not be qualified by a half-conscious desire to impress or enlighten others. Keep your journal private and in a secure place. The time will come later to share your insights and breakthroughs—after spiritual understanding and experience have become a significant and solid part of your own life.

———

WHEN YOU READ INFORMATION somewhere that seems particularly insightful to you, copy it into your journal. The added emphasis it gets by the close attention during the act of copying will help clarify it to your consciousness. What you copy will prove still more useful if you translate it into your own words as you enter it into your journal, being careful, of course, not to miss its point or change its meaning. Once it's written in your most private book, it becomes available again and again to refresh your memory.

When you have a meaningful meditation or special insight, record the gist of it in your journal, perhaps, in the process, relating it to something you've previously read or experienced. Remember, the goal is to develop a deep and overall grasp, an informed understanding. Copy, compose, compare— whatever works to deepen your clarity. There is both a great discipline and a reward associated with working at a core idea until it's perfectly clear to you and has become your own. Writing out your insights and the unfolding of new realizations about ultimate spiritual realities as they come to you is so helpful that the practice can be considered almost essential. I have found it to be extremely helpful to me and to most others with whom I've worked.

———

PERHAPS A PERSON becomes completely convinced of the importance and worth of spiritual journaling only after experiencing what a help it proves to be over a period of time. Try to trust that this importance is real. Go buy yourself a notebook that appeals to you, and start writing. You're off on a great adventure, and this notebook is the log for your journey to a fulfillment and happiness you cannot as yet even imagine.